MADE IN SPAIN

*Recipes and stories from
my country and beyond*

Miriam González
Durántez

HODDER &
STOUGHTON

To my grandmother María, who taught me that the least important thing when cooking is the food

CONTENTS

Introduction 09

Soup 18

Tapas 40

Eggs 62

Salads and vegetables 76

Fish 112

Meat 142

Comfort food and one-pot meals 172

A bit of fun 196

Snacks 202

Fruit 222

Desserts and baking 244

Index 274

Introduction

This book is about my personal journey through food: how cooking has kept me anchored to my Spanish roots, and to my family and friends; how it has helped me to go through the intense political years of the coalition government without losing my mind; and, ultimately, how food is a strong link between my children and myself, as well as between them and my home country and family.

When we began writing the mumandsons blog in January 2012, my objective was to get my children (three boys) to learn about food and cooking. It all started as a temporary project, as we decided we would stop the blog as soon as we raised £60. Four years on, we are still running the blog, partly out of success – because we enjoy the cooking – and partly out of miserable failure as, believe it or not, we have not yet reached our £60 target! (So much, at least in my household, for the magic of the internet.)

Still, we now have a shade under 300 recipes – most of them Spanish, or at least Spanish inspired – on the blog, a fair number of hits per week, we have received an award, and one of my sons is becoming a real food connoisseur. So far, so good.

While I hope the blog has helped all my sons to share my love of Spanish food and to feel more connected to Spain, the recipes on the blog – and in this book – are not solely Spanish: they reflect my particular life journey, and therefore include a few British and international recipes I have come to love on the way.

By publishing this book, I also hope to raise funds to help me lead Inspiring Girls, an international campaign that I am launching to get female role models talking to girls all over the world, building partly on the success of the Inspiring Women campaign in the UK, but using technology so that we can connect inspirational women from all walks of life with girls, no matter where they come from or where they are.

My children have helped with the photos, some of which are here in these pages. (They may not be quite as good as professional food photography yet, but I like to think they give a sense of the food as it is cooked and eaten at our home.) I may or may not manage to teach my children to cook with the blog and this book. But I certainly want my sons to learn to be able to distinguish good food from bad food, to know which flavours work well together and which do not, and – especially – I want them to gain a respect for good ingredients. In a nutshell, I want my children to have the chance to truly enjoy food, from Spain and elsewhere, as much as I do. Because enjoying food is enjoying life.

Back to my roots

I am an immigrant. I came to live in the UK on a hot summer evening in late June 2005. I remember it well, because I had fought against coming here for at least two years before that. Partly because, as a mum of (then) two young sons, London seemed daunting to me; and partly because coming here meant giving up my job as an adviser to the European Foreign Affairs Commissioner, a job that I was passionate about. I arrived on my own: my husband Nick was in his constituency in Sheffield; our children were with my family in Spain while we got installed; and the removal van with our furniture got lost (hard to believe, I know!) on the way to the UK. As a result, I spent a few days on my own just wandering around London with nothing else to do.

By the time Nick (and the furniture) arrived, I was already in love with the city. Ever since then, I get deeply offended whenever anybody makes the tiniest critical remark – even if justified – about London. I am convinced that if we could bottle and sell the energy that you feel in London, it would become a best-selling product worldwide. I simply do not know any other place that offers the same sense of freedom and possibility.

And yet, much as I hero-worship this country, I am deeply Spanish. I have been asked endlessly (by journalists) why I do not acquire British nationality, especially as it would mean that I could vote at general elections. The answer is very simple: I cannot change my nationality, because being Spanish is who I am.

Me as a baby

Me with my father

Me as a little girl in very traditional Spanish clothes

Me with my mother

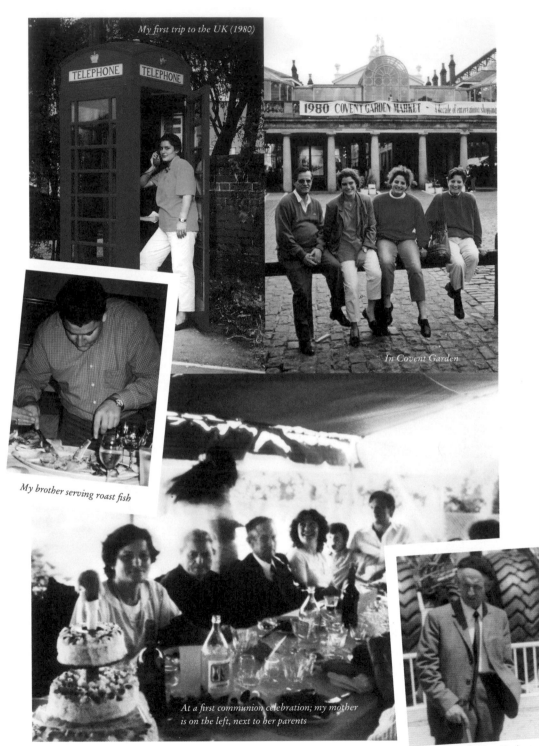

My first trip to the UK (1980)

1980 COVENT GARDEN MARKET

In Covent Garden

My brother serving roast fish

At a first communion celebration; my mother is on the left, next to her parents

My grandfather, Mariano

I was born at a time of dictatorship in Spain. I come from a village in the middle of the country, called Olmedo, where we all know each other. My mother was a science teacher at the local secondary school and my father was mayor of the village for almost 20 years. They were both the first people in their farming families who went to university. They were also truly blessed, because they lived during a period of intense social mobility, so my father (who had had to enrol in the Catholic church to become a priest so that he would be able to get an education) managed to make it all the way up to senator. I was lucky that he left the Catholic church or else I would not have been born!

It pains me to say it, because it reminds me of my age, but until I was eight years old, women in my home country could not own a bank current account and could not travel abroad without the permission of their husbands and fathers. Spain has changed beyond recognition, not only economically but socially as well: these days there is very little class divide, women are treated as equal, it was one of the first European countries to recognise gay marriage... There are very few other countries in the world that can boast such a proud record of modernisation and stability. Spain is a confident and open country that endlessly reinvents itself, no matter what the difficulties.

About the only thing that old and new Spain have in common, the thing that over the years has remained the same no matter what the ups and downs of the country on the world stage, is our love of food. Food is at the centre of everything we do. It is almost an obsession. As we eat breakfast we think about what we will have for lunch, and during lunch we discuss what we will serve for dinner. We look for and treasure good-quality ingredients as if they were gold; we take the tiniest criticism of our food more seriously than any national threat; and, deep down, we feel real pity for the countries that have worse food than us... which in our book is pretty much every one of them! Chauvinistic, I know, but still true.

In Spanish families, when you have eaten a really good home-made meal, people stay at the table after the meal has ended, chatting and putting the world to rights. It is called the *sobremesa*, which literally means 'over the table'. Pretty much all the memories of my childhood that I treasure are linked to *sobremesas*. It was during *sobremesas* that my grandfather told us the stories of my family; that he brain-washed me and my sister about 'economic independence being the key to happiness'; that we shared the family achievements and also our preoccupations; that my mother told us about foreign countries and we planned trips with her; that the virus of politics got into my blood as my father shared with us the events of the day during the Spanish transition to democracy...

In true Spanish fashion, *sobremesas* are emotionally charged times. We never go light on emotion in Spain! During the *sobremesas* we tighten family bonds and forge wonderful friendships, but we also have monumentally loud arguments. We do not even have to care too much about any subject, the key is just to disagree: from heated discussions about politics, to the pros and cons of bull-fighting; from the role of religion in the country, to arguments about who cooks best (just in case you are wondering, the answer to this must always be: 'my mum').

Many of the recipes of this book are for food that will make you want to remain at the table long after you have eaten it. They are recipes that have been cooked by my mother and, before her, my grandmother, and are now eaten by me with 'my four men': Nick and my sons. They are the dishes that over the years have provided us with endless occasions for good *sobremesas*, whether on our own or with friends. I hope you enjoy them as much as we do and that you, too, will argue, make up and form happy memories over these recipes.

My father greeting a (very young) king of Spain

The house of my maternal grandparents, with the farm at the back and fruit trees – apples, pears and chestnuts – at the front

Ham for sale in a market

Me with my uncle... and a lot of seafood!

The church of Santa Maria in my village, where Nick and I got married

A view of my village

Though globalisation has left as much of a mark on Spain as it has everywhere else, the one bit of the Spanish culture that is totally impermeable to interference from the outside world is the pattern and timing of meals. Breakfast is often coffee and biscuits (bizarre, and unhealthy as well!). Then comes a copious lunch at 2.30 or 3pm. And we round off the day with a lighter dinner that normally starts between 9.30 and 10pm. Most restaurants do not even open before 9pm, and that is regardless of whether you go there on your own or with kids. In fact you will struggle to find restaurants 'for kids' in Spain; we just bring children to all restaurants and miraculously they seem to adapt to it.

These are some examples of menus that any Spanish family would eat. You normally have a first course of vegetables, soup or eggs and a main dish of fish or meat. Dessert is often an orange in winter (Spanish oranges are at their best around Christmas time) and melon or watermelon in summer. However, if we have a celebration, we serve a dessert as well.

Typically Spanish menus

Lunch for a winter day	*Lunch or dinner for a summer day*
Bolitas soup *(see page 32)*	*Gazpacho (see page 29)*
–	–
Hake in green sauce *(see page 120)*	Roast fish *(see page 136)*
–	–
Flan *(see page 253)*	A slice of watermelon

*Lunch for a
'comfort food day'*

A bowl of *Lentejas (see page 21)*

–

A couple of Russian steaks
(see page 152)

–

An orange 'to get rid of the fat',
as Spaniards often say

Lunch for a Sunday

Salmorejo (see page 39)

–

A dish of Ibérico ham to share

–

And a generous portion of *Marmitako
(see page 117)*… with a large glass of
cold white wine

*Lunch or dinner
for a celebration day*

A bowl of Fish soup *(see page 22)*

–

My grandma's
Partridges *estofadas (see page 150)*

–

And a tiny but heavenly
portion of *Leche frita (see page 246)*

SOUP

Gazpacho seems to be the only Spanish soup that most people outside the country associate with Spain; it's undeniably a good dish, but there are many more options than that.

A soup that every single person in Spain eats many times during the winter is *lentejas*. A good bowl of *lentejas* (lentils) is simply the flavour of home. The same goes for *bolitas* soup (aka *sopa de cocido*); a single spoonful of this brothy pasta serves to make most Spaniards nostalgic about their childhood.

Gazpacho, on the other hand, is for summer. No Spanish person will touch *gazpacho* unless it is a seriously hot day (and hot really means hot in Spain). The same goes for *salmorejo*, which is not as well known as *gazpacho*, but is much better… in my humble opinion.

Most Spanish soups (indeed, most Spanish stews) require a bay leaf. It is important that you remember to remove the bay leaf before serving any soup as, in Spain, finding a bay leaf in your bowl means you will be cursed with not getting married… I bet you, at a good many weddings, some mothers-in-law secretly wish they had served their children more bay leaves!

Lentejas

This is my universal cure-all during the winter: if my children are upset; if something goes wrong at work; if you are feeling down... my usual response is, 'come here and I'll make you some *lentejas*'. It will not make the bad stuff disappear, but somehow it will seem less of a problem when you discuss it with your family over a bowl of good, homely food.

Most families in Spain eat *lentejas* once a week during the winter. It is hearty but also very healthy... and cheap, too. In the past it would have been a first course, followed by fish or meat. Now that everybody is so health-conscious, it is normally eaten as a meal on its own.

Lentejas was one of my father's favourite dishes. He used to pour a spoonful of red wine vinegar on top of the *lentejas* and that is what I now do, too. My children prefer shreds of chorizo on top of theirs, either fried in a dry pan or just chopped and microwaved on a high setting (I use a 700W oven) for 45 seconds.

You may be able to find the Pardina lentils I use in a delicatessen or Spanish shop or – of course – online; otherwise Puy lentils are fine for this.

Serves 4

250g Pardina or Puy lentils
2 tbsp olive oil
1 leek, finely sliced
½ red pepper and ½ green pepper
   (no need to slice them)
2 carrots, finely chopped

4 garlic cloves, finely sliced
sea salt
1 bay leaf
½ tsp sweet smoked paprika (*pimentón*)
a few parsley leaves, finely chopped

In the morning, a few hours before you are going to make the dish, soak the lentils in a large bowl of cold water. (This is not essential, but try to find a few moments to do it, as it will help.) When you are ready to cook, drain the lentils.

Heat a large pan over a medium-high heat and add the olive oil. When the oil is hot, add all the ingredients and fry them for four to five minutes. Add enough water to just cover everything. Let it come to the boil, then reduce the heat, cover and simmer for 45–50 minutes until the lentils are tender. If you make this in a pressure cooker (I like things fast, so I use this a lot), it will be ready in just 20 minutes.

Take out the peppers and about half a cup of lentils. Blend these until smooth, with a hand-held or free-standing blender. Return the blended mixture to the pan and mix it well with the rest of the lentils. That is all there is to it.

Remember to get rid of that bay leaf...

Fish soup

This is a delicate soup, the kind of dish that Spanish mothers used to prepare for festive meals or the occasional Sunday. During my childhood, on a fish soup type of day, it was also imperative to dress nicely. Even today, in my home village, people wear their Sunday best. Whether this is a sign of religious respect, or just a chance to show off your best clothes while promenading to church, God only knows... When I see some women in my village walking to church wrapped in huge fur coats while the temperature is 20°C, I have doubts myself!

My mother prepares this often for my children. Leave out the clams if your children aren't keen on them.

A handy tip to remove any sand from clams is to put them in a large bowl of cold salty water (about 1 litre of water and a handful of salt). Leave them there for a couple of hours (in the fridge if it is a hot day). Though I cannot explain the physics of how it works, all the sand will sink to the bottom of the bowl.

To make fish stock, just simmer 3 litres of water with 3 flat fish bones, ½ onion and 1 bay leaf for 30 minutes, then strain the liquid. You can also use prawn shells, or fish heads. Don't feel you have to make stock though; water will do just fine.

Serves 4

2 tbsp olive oil, plus more
  for the prawns
1 onion, chopped
1 celery stick, chopped
1 carrot, chopped
1 garlic clove, finely chopped
½ red pepper and ½ yellow
  pepper, chopped
1 potato, chopped

1 fillet of white fish (haddock, monkfish,
  cod, hake...)
sea salt
½ tsp finely chopped parsley leaves
1 bay leaf
1 squid (frozen is fine here)
handful of raw prawns, peeled
  and deveined
handful of clams (optional)

Heat a large pan over a medium-high heat and add the olive oil. When the oil is hot, add all the vegetables. After five minutes (when they start turning brown), reduce the heat so that they soften. When they are soft – after another five to eight minutes – add the white fish. Let the fish fry with the vegetables for three or four minutes, or until it is just cooked, then take it out and set aside. Add the salt, parsley and bay leaf. Pour in 900ml of water or fish stock, bring to the boil, then reduce the heat and simmer for 10–15 minutes.

Take the bay leaf out, return the white fish and liquidise it all with a hand-held blender, or in a food processor, until you have a smooth soup.

Separately heat a frying pan. Cut the squid into small squares, add them to the dry pan and, as soon as they harden (one or two minutes), add them to the soup. Cut the prawns into small pieces. Heat a tiny bit of oil in the frying pan, then add the prawns. Stir for one or two minutes until they turn a coral colour, then add to the soup.

Finally, add some water to the frying pan, about half a glass (75ml) should do. Scrub the clams and discard any with cracked shells, or that are open and do not close when tapped sharply against the sink. Add the clams, cover and wait for a couple of minutes until they open up. Discard any that do not open. Remove most of the clams from their shells and add them all to the soup. Strain their cooking liquid through a sieve (in case they have given out any sand or grit) and add this to the soup, too. Stir and serve.

Garlic soup

My grandfather on my mother's side, Mariano Durántez, was a real character; a curious self-made and completely self-taught man who had received only a rudimentary education in rural Spain. For a little girl, as I was at the time, he was a real Titan, and I spent most summers at his village just hanging around with him. These are some of the things I remember him for:

He believed in empirical science and learned things just through experience: he knew for example at any moment of the day what time it was simply because of the position of the sun.

He knew the names of every crop, every single tree and most stars.

He was the person with the strongest will I have ever met: he had lost a leg in an accident while hunting on a horse, yet he was as agile with one leg as anybody else is with two.

He read voraciously and was a subscriber to two publications: El Palentino, *the local newspaper of his region, and* Reader's Digest*... don't ask me why.*

He was an entrenched Catholic and yet he hated the church with passion.

He was really good at carpentry and building (he built his own house) and our proudest achievement together was building the loo when running water finally came to his village (yes, building a loo from scratch was probably one of the finest moments of my youth. And no, I do not feel any embarrassment at all about that).

He did not do a single household chore during his whole life as he thought they were 'female tasks', yet he pushed my mum to get a physics and chemistry degree and he brain-washed me and my sister about economic independence being the key to happiness, to the point I feel that it is engraved on my DNA.

... So when people accuse me of being full of contradictions I suppose I should say: 'Look at my grandfather!'

As far as food was concerned, he never ate a shop-made cake, he had the same dinner every single day of his life – two soft-boiled eggs ('just five minutes, no more no less') and a garlic soup – and drank two glasses of red wine, one for lunch and one for dinner, every day of his adult life. It must be a healthy diet because he lived until he was 96.

This is the garlic soup, very typical of the Castilian region, that I can cook with my eyes closed after preparing it so many times for him. And a Spanish cook's tip from me, too: if you dislike the smell of garlic on your hands, put them under the cold water tap and let the water run *without rubbing them*. The odour should dissipate within seconds.

Serves 1

2 tbsp olive oil
2 garlic cloves, very finely chopped
25g Serrano or Parma ham, finely chopped (optional)
1 tsp sweet smoked paprika (*pimentón*)
sea salt
1 egg
some coarse-textured stale bread, torn into pieces

Boil a kettle of water. Put the olive oil in a saucepan with the garlic and place over a medium heat. If you are using the ham, add it now and let it fry for a couple of minutes. When the garlic is about to become golden (two minutes maximum), add the paprika. Let it fry for 10 seconds, then pour in 500ml of hot water from the kettle and add the salt. As soon as the soup starts to boil, let it simmer for three to five minutes and then take it off the heat.

Beat the egg and pour it slowly over the soup while stirring constantly. Then add the stale bread and serve. In our family we do not like the bread too soft, but if you prefer it this way you can let the soup simmer for a final five minutes.

My maternal grandfather, Mariano Durántez

Garden soup

When I was little, Spanish kids used to be served this soup at least every other week. It is a very good way to get children to eat veggies, though in principle I am against the movement that 'hides' vegetables in food so that children eat them without fuss. Much better, in my view, to get them to see the vegetables, recognise them and become progressively used to their flavours. They may dislike them at first but, if you are half as stubborn as I am (and I'm assuming you may find reaching my level of stubbornness challenging), you will surely get there.

If you are feeling lazy, just buy a bag of ready-chopped vegetables at the supermarket, though that will increase the cost. You can get this soup made in 15–20 minutes and it makes a nice lunch almost on its own.

Serves 4–6

olive oil
1 carrot, finely chopped
1 celery stick, finely chopped
1 leek or 1 onion, finely chopped
1 bay leaf
1 litre chicken or vegetable stock (or, if you cannot be bothered, just water)
pinch of sea salt
½ tsp sweet smoked paprika (*pimentón*)
3 handfuls of small pasta (vermicelli, or small stars or snails)

Cover the base of a large saucepan with a thin layer of olive oil and place over a medium heat. Add all the vegetables and the bay leaf and cook, stirring occasionally, until they are soft and golden. This will take five or six minutes.

Pour in the stock or water, then add the salt and the paprika. Increase the heat to high and bring it to the boil.

Once it is boiling, add the pasta and cook until soft, following the instructions on the packet (vermicelli needs only three or four minutes). I like the vegetables crunchy and the pasta soft, but if you prefer the pasta al dente you can alter the cooking time as you wish.

As my eldest says: '*de-li-cio-so*'!

Gazpacho

This Spanish classic is a regular at any of my dinners when the weather is properly hot. You can prepare it hours in advance, as it needs to be well chilled.

As with any soup, it requires minimal motor skills when eating… or at least minimal social skills if you spill it. At our dinner table, we once had a senior Secretary of the Government pour this all over his very white shirt… and he was so very awkward about it that he did not say a thing and spent the whole dinner (and bear in mind that this was only the first course) pretending that the massive stains on his shirt just did not exist. So, in turn, and in order to not embarrass him further, we avoided looking at those humungous stains for the entire, long duration of the dinner. The only way to do this is to fix your gaze on your guest's eyes and never lower your sights. Unfortunately, all we could think about for the rest of the dinner was precisely those stains, exactly like when you are starting to date somebody and during your first dinner together they get spinach stuck in their teeth…

Serves 4

1 cucumber, peeled
7 ripe tomatoes
½ onion
½ green pepper
1 garlic clove
1 glass of good olive oil (about 150ml)
2–3 tbsp red wine vinegar, to taste
sea salt, to taste (but remember that tomatoes take a lot of salt)

Cut the vegetables in big chunks, put them all in a beaker, add half a glass (about 75ml) of water and blend with a hand-held blender, or a free-standing blender or food processor, until they are liquidised. Add the oil, vinegar and salt and blend again until the oil emulsifies. Push it all through a sieve, cover and put it in the fridge for at least one hour. If it is too thick for you, just add more water.

You can serve this with neat little cubes of cucumber, red pepper, hard-boiled egg whites or fried or toasted bread. If the weather is very hot, add some ice cubes before serving it, too.

My children love this. It is the easiest way to get them to eat lots of raw vegetables.

Courgette soup

We peel the courgettes for this in our family, only because the children prefer it not to be 'too green', but if you don't mind the colour then leave some or all of the skins on.

My theory (yes, I have reached an age when it is actually fine to have theories about these things) is that what puts people off cooking home-made soups is the question of stock. Stock was surely invented to persuade people not to cook. I am not prone to conspiracy theories, but I bet you it is big food companies who have been convincing chefs to say that you need stock to make soup.

Picture the scene: You come home late, fry a few courgettes and leeks, add water, let it boil while you grill some fish or meat, blend the soup with a hand-held blender and, there you go, dinner in less than 20 minutes.

Now, what about this: You come home late, think of making a soup, fry a few courgettes and leeks and then have to find stock… and this is what happens: you curse yourself for not having planned that you wanted to eat soup in advance, in which case you should have bought the ingredients for the stock – and prepared it as well – the day before you actually planned to eat the soup, or otherwise wait for 45 minutes while the stock is being cooked (that is provided you already have the ingredients) before you even get to preparing the soup… even thinking about it stresses me out. You could of course buy ready-made stock, but then what is the point of home-made soup?

Stock is good if cooking a special meal, but for every day, water will do just fine.

Serves 4

1 tbsp olive oil
2 leeks, cut into not-too-thin slices
5 courgettes, peeled if you prefer, cut into not-too-small chunks
sea salt
shaved or finely grated Parmesan cheese, to serve (optional)

Heat the oil in a deep saucepan over a high heat. Add the leeks and fry for five minutes, then add the courgettes and the salt and fry for another five minutes.

Pour in 500ml of boiling water, reduce the heat and simmer for 15 minutes. Finally, blend the soup with a hand-held blender, or in a free-standing blender or a food processor. Add more boiling water if you want it to be thinner.

Serve on its own, or with Parmesan cheese scattered over.

Bolitas soup

This wintry dish is actually called *sopa de cocido* in Spain. It is heaven and the kitchen smells divine when you are cooking it. We call it *bolitas* because, in Spain, it is normally prepared with tiny balls of pasta that look a bit like couscous. If you cannot find those in the shops, little stars are great, too.

My mother Mercedes, who is a very good cook, thinks that this soup is the solution to most illnesses, whether physical or mental. Since she is a chemistry and physics teacher with a totally scientific approach to life, I bet you it is true. She leaves no room for sentimentality when it comes to food... or anything else. Once the children told her that they had heard about some people who claimed to have seen an apparition of the Virgin Mary and she solemnly declared, 'That is because they do not eat well!'

It is not worth spending a lot on the meat for this soup; just ask for any leftover scraps of a ham at the supermarket – the bone is actually very good for this – and use any stewing beef. Ideally soak the chickpeas overnight, though it is no drama if you forget, as you will be discarding them after cooking in any case.

Serves 4–6

leftovers from a roast chicken,
  including the bones, or a chicken
  leg (thigh and drumstick together)
200g Serrano ham, scraps or a bone
150g stewing beef, such as chuck
  or shin
handful of dried chickpeas, ideally
  soaked overnight
1 onion, chopped

1 leek, in big chunks
1 carrot, in big chunks
6 green beans, in big chunks (optional)
1 bay leaf
¼ green or red pepper, in big chunks
½ tsp parsley leaves
sea salt
tiny star-shaped pasta, 1 handful
  for every 2 people

Put all the ingredients but the pasta into a very large saucepan and pour in two litres of water. Bring to the boil, then reduce the heat to its lowest setting and let it all simmer for two hours (if you do this in a pressure cooker, one hour will be enough).

Push the soup though a colander and get rid of all the solid bits (if you have used proper chicken rather than leftovers you can pick out the meat and use it in a salad). This broth keeps, covered, for a week or so in the fridge.

When you want to eat it, return the broth to the boil (if you find the taste too strong, add more water), add the pasta and cook until soft, following the instructions on the packet.

Potatoes with chorizo

This is a straightforward winter (read: heavy) lunch meal. It originally comes from the Rioja region, best-known for its red wines, and is correctly called *patatas a la riojana*.

Wine is almost a matter of religion in Spain and we get seriously offended if we are told that French wines (or for that matter any other wines) might be better than ours. My husband could not stop giggling the first time he saw a friend of mine opening a bottle of Vega Sicilia and pompously declaring that it was 'the best wine in the world'. My village is in Valladolid, near the Ribera del Duero region, where we produce some of the best wines in the country (some of it is exported, but normally not the good vintages). Regardless of Nick's giggles and my friend's pomposity, Vega Sicilia is truly one of the best wines in the world (and 1970 Vega Sicilia Unico probably the very best, I think). What is certain is that you will need a glass of wine to digest this dish!

Try to buy good-quality chorizo, as cheap versions tend to be full of fat.

Serves 2 for lunch

2 tbsp olive oil
1 garlic clove, finely sliced
1 onion, finely sliced
150g chorizo, cut in 1cm slices
250g potatoes, cut in chunks
sea salt
1 bay leaf
1 tbsp sweet smoked paprika (*pimentón*)

Heat the olive oil in a large frying pan over a medium-low heat, just to warm the oil. Add the garlic and wait for a minute or so until it is golden. Then add the onion, reduce the heat and let it fry for 10 minutes until translucent and a little golden. Then add the chorizo and cook for 10 minutes (if you want less fat, heat the chorizo for 30 seconds in a microwave on a high setting first – I use a 700W oven – then drain it to get rid of all the fat before adding to the pan).

Add the potatoes and continue frying over a medium heat for 10 minutes. Add the salt, bay leaf and paprika and cover the whole lot with about 500ml of water, or however much it takes to cover the potatoes. Return to the boil, then reduce the heat to a simmer and cook for 20 minutes, until the potatoes are soft and the soup around them has thickened.

Lent chickpeas

A traditional Spanish soup for Easter. It is often made with salted cod, but this vegetarian version is also very good. Originally this was eaten on Fridays during Lent as – Spain being a Catholic country – it was forbidden to eat meat... a sign of the old times when meat was more expensive (thus more of a luxury) than fish. If you want to try the cod version, soak 150g of salted cod for 48 hours (change the water three times), then cut it into chunks and add it to the soup for the last seven minutes of cooking time.

Although the practice of Catholicism has faded in Spain, people continue to make this soup, just as we keep other traditions, from the truly impressive (such as the processions at Easter), to the sentimental (decorating the streets with flowers during Corpus Christi), to the plain weird (such as throwing bread and cheese at the image of the local saint in some villages).

Serves 4

200g dried chickpeas
sea salt
1 carrot
2 onions, 1 whole, 1 finely sliced
1 bay leaf
3 tbsp olive oil
1 garlic clove, very finely chopped
½ tsp ground cumin
1 tsp sweet smoked paprika (*pimentón*)
200g spinach
whites from 2 hard-boiled eggs

The night before you prepare this, soak the chickpeas in cold water (cover them completely) and leave them overnight. The following morning, drain off the water.

Put the chickpeas in a saucepan, add boiling water just to cover (probably about 300ml), salt, the whole (peeled) carrot, whole onion and bay leaf. Simmer for 1½–1¾ hours, until the chickpeas are tender.

Meanwhile, heat the olive oil in a frying pan over a low heat, add the sliced onion and garlic and let it fry for 10-ish minutes until soft. Then add the cumin, paprika and spinach leaves. Wait for a couple of minutes, turning once or twice, until the spinach leaves wilt. When the chickpeas are ready, tip in the contents of the frying pan. Then chop the whites of the hard-boiled eggs and add them to the pan, too.

This tastes better the day after you have cooked it, when the flavours have had a chance to meld together.

One of the many processions, this one to honour San Antonio, in my father's village

Salmorejo

This is a really easy way to get children to eat tomatoes. It is a very typical cold soup from the south of Spain, a bit like a thick *gazpacho*, except that the 'king' of *gazpacho* is the cucumber, while the 'king' of *salmorejo* is the tomato. My children eat this as a cold soup in the summer, but they also like it on top of crusty bread, preferably with a bit of ham on top. (Or try it with aubergines, see page 210.)

It is also a nice recipe to make with children as they seem to particularly enjoy squeezing the tomatoes and the bread, which is indeed a very satisfactory feeling. And blending soup is always something younger kids seem to like. Leaving the tomatoes 'to rest' with the bread and garlic is a tip from my sister, who understands tomatoes better than anybody else in my family.

Serves 4–6

1kg tomatoes, as red and ripe as possible, quartered
200g stale baguette-type bread, torn
200ml olive oil
2 garlic cloves
sea salt
red wine vinegar

Put the tomatoes in a bowl with the bread, the olive oil and the peeled garlic cloves. Mix it all well with your hands, squeezing the tomatoes a bit. Cover the bowl with cling film and let it marinate for at least three hours.

Fish out and throw away the garlic cloves and blend all the other ingredients with a hand-held blender, or in a free-standing blender or food processor. Push the mixture through a sieve to make it smooth, then add salt and vinegar to taste. (If you plan to serve it as a soup, rather than a dip or spread, you may want to thin it out a bit with 250ml of water.) Serve the soup in bowls, or the thicker version with little bits of cured ham, or with chopped hard-boiled egg, or just on its own.

TAPAS

Tapas is probably the most misunderstood concept of Spanish cuisine. Though there are many theories about the origin of tapas, the one that is most often heard is that they started life as morsels placed on slices of bread that, in turn, were used as 'lids' to cover glasses of beer across the country, to keep flies off. (We definitely have a lot of flies in Spain!)

Ir de tapas (going for tapas) in Spain has nothing to do with going to a restaurant for a meal made up of lots of little dishes, which is what it means in Britain. We just do not do that in Spain. Instead, it means going from bar to bar, having a glass of wine or beer with a tiny bit of food (a tapa) in each of them. We keep moving as we eat and drink, meeting people in the bars and the street as we go, which means that *ir de tapas* is essentially a social occasion, rather than a sit-down meal. Tapas is all about the street, not about the restaurant or bar.

Going '*de tapas*' in places such as Triana in Seville, the Casco Viejo in San Sebastián, or Correos near my home town in Valladolid, is the closest you can get to the essence of Spanish life.

Here are some tapas recipes you can easily find in most Spanish towns.

Croquetas

This is a very traditional Spanish snack. It is 'left over' food, originally made with the scraps from a roast chicken, or what could be salvaged from the chicken or ham bones that you boil for a soup. This recipe is made with Serrano ham and I think they are the best, but *croquetas* are also delicious with the same amount of chicken, or 200g raw prawns, or four hard-boiled eggs. They are cheap to make but, like other economical home-made foods, they have now become a bit of a delicacy at glamorous restaurants.

I am a very impatient person, so I rarely find the serenity to make *croquetas*, which also explains why I do not do yoga, bird watching, train spotting or meditation. But if you have a disposition that tends towards repetitive tasks and contemplation, making *croquetas* is definitely for you.

Two of my aunts are my family's queens of *croquetas*. They make bags of them, freeze them and give them to all of us when they come to visit which is great, because, as a result, we have supplies in the freezer for more than a year. The only disadvantage is that the two aunts tend to compete with each other, so when you try their *croquetas* you had better tell them that they are the very best, or they will not be impressed.

Unluckily for my aunts, they do not get any public credit for the *croquetas*, as for some reason when the Spanish media write about Nick – or when they interview me – they keep referring to him loving 'my mother's *croquetas*'. I've no idea where they got this from, as my mother – who is as impatient as I am – has not made a single *croqueta* since I was 10. Still, if you are married to a Spanish woman and you are asked whether you like the *croquetas* of your mother-in-law (*las croquetas de la suegra*), you're meant to say yes, no matter whether she makes them or not! The *suegra* is always right.

It can be tricky to mould the béchamel if you are not used to it. You could of course make the mixture easier to handle by adding more flour, but do try to avoid that: these are supposed to be creamy and unctuous inside.

Makes 45–50

For the croquetas
4 tbsp olive oil, plus more to deep-fry
1 leek, finely chopped
75g plain flour
1 litre whole or semi-skimmed milk
300g Serrano or Parma ham, very
    finely chopped (you can do this
    in a food processor)
sea salt
pinch of freshly grated nutmeg
2 slices of mild Cheddar cheese, or
    Edam, Gouda and so on

*To coat (these are approximate amounts;
    add more if needed)*
1 glass of plain flour
1 beaten egg, mixed with 3 tbsp milk
1 glass of fine breadcrumbs

Continued overleaf…

Heat the 4 tbsp of oil in a deep saucepan over a medium heat. Add the leek, reduce the heat and cook it for 10 minutes until it becomes translucent. Stir in the flour and continue stirring for five minutes until the flour is golden. Separately (in the microwave if you wish) warm the milk, then gradually pour it into the flour mixture, while stirring, to make a smooth sauce. Cook, stirring continuously, for about two minutes. Take the pan off the heat. Now, this is the trick for smooth velvety *croquetas*: with a hand-held blender, blend the mixture well for three or four minutes.

Add the ham, salt and nutmeg. Return to the heat and keep stirring until you have a thick sauce; this should take another four minutes, more or less. As you take the pan off the heat, add the cheese. It should melt immediately. Stir it all once more, pour into a shallow dish and let it cool for at least one hour (or overnight).

Place three dishes in a row. Pour the flour for coating into the first. Pour the beaten egg and milk into the second. Tip the breadcrumbs into the last.

Take a spoonful of the *croquetas* mixture (it should not be too sticky; if it is, let it cool for a bit longer). With your hands, mould the mixture into an almond shape or cylinder. Keep doing this with the rest of the mixture to make 45–50 *croquetas*.

Roll the *croquetas* in the flour, then in the egg and milk, and finally in the breadcrumbs. Put them on a tray (they should not touch each other) and place in the fridge to firm up. They are even better if you freeze them at this point, again on the tray, then decant them – once frozen solid – into freezer bags; they will keep well for two to three months in the freezer.

In a deep saucepan or deep-fat fryer, heat about 10cm of olive oil over a high heat. The oil should not come more than halfway up the sides of the pan. Add five or six *croquetas* (you need to fry them in batches). Reduce the heat to medium and fry for two or three minutes, turning once, until golden. Remove with a slotted spoon, placing on a tray lined with kitchen paper to blot off the excess oil. Serve immediately.

I do not know any children who do not like *croquetas*.

Tigres

In a really clever move, many years ago, one of my '*croquetas* aunts' decided to get some competitive advantage by preparing *tigres*, which is the mussels version of *croquetas*. She now cooks them always when we go to Spain, which is lucky because these little things are truly laborious to make, but the children love them. You may prefer these to *croquetas*... but, if you do, please don't tell my other aunt!

Makes 20

For the tigres
20 mussels
1½ onions, finely chopped
¼ green pepper, finely chopped
1 garlic clove, finely chopped
4 tbsp olive oil, plus more to deep-fry
8 raw prawns, peeled, deveined and
    finely chopped
sea salt
75g plain flour
850ml whole or semi-skimmed milk

To coat (these are approximate amounts;
    add more if needed)
1 glass of plain flour
2 beaten eggs, mixed with 3 tbsp milk
1 glass of fine breadcrumbs

Clean the mussels by scrubbing and removing the 'beards' and prising off any barnacles with a table knife. Discard any that are cracked, or that are open and do not close when sharply tapped against the side of the sink. Put half a glass of water (about 75ml) in a saucepan. When the pan is hot, add the mussels and cover. As soon as they open up, take them off the heat and discard any that remain closed. Then strain their cooking liquid through a sieve (in case they have given out any sand or grit). Take the mussels out of their shells, break each shell at the hinge and put the half-shells aside. Cut the mussels into small pieces.

In a separate pan, fry the onions, green pepper and garlic in 2 tbsp of the olive oil until the onion becomes translucent (12–15 minutes). Then add the prawns and mussels and cook for a couple of minutes more. Add salt and remove from the heat.

Separately prepare the béchamel: heat another 2 tbsp of the olive oil, add the 75g of flour and let it get hot for two or three minutes, stirring well. Separately (in the microwave if you wish) warm the milk, then gradually pour it into the flour mixture, while stirring, to make a smooth sauce. Cook, stirring continuously, for about two minutes.

Take the pan off the heat. Blend with a hand-held blender for three or four minutes, then return it to the heat until it bubbles and thickens, stirring constantly. Add 4 tbsp of the mussel cooking liquid, then the mussels mixture. Divide between the best-looking mussel half-shells and let them cool (discard any remaining shells).

Put three dishes in a row. Pour the flour for coating into the first. Pour the beaten eggs and milk into the second. Tip the breadcrumbs into the last.

Dust the sauce side of the shells with flour, then dip them into the eggs. Finally, coat them with the crumbs.

In a deep saucepan or deep-fat fryer, heat about 10cm of olive oil (a lot of it!) over a high heat. The oil should not come more than halfway up the sides of the pan. Fry the *tigres* in small batches for a couple of minutes, turning once, until golden. Remove with a slotted spoon, placing on a tray lined with kitchen paper to blot off the excess oil. Serve immediately.

Little salad *Ensaladilla*

This is one of the foods that ex-pat Spaniards miss most; just bring them to any bar mid-morning when they are back in Spain and they will always ask for *ensaladilla*. The best way to eat it is with bread. I know you are thinking that bread, potatoes and mayonnaise is not a healthy combination, and you are right… but once you are at this point, just give up and add a very cold beer as well.

Serves 4

2 large potatoes
2 carrots
6 green beans
sea salt
2 eggs
160g can of tuna

8 green olives, pitted
8 pickles (acidic such as cornichons,
   not sweet pickles)
4 canned red peppers (preferably piquillo)
300ml mayonnaise (shop-bought or
   home-made, see right)

Cut the potatoes, carrots and beans into small cubes and tip them into boiling salted water, cooking until they are tender. We boil them separately so that the flavours do not mix, but if you don't have time, just cook them together. It should take 10 minutes for the potatoes and the carrots and eight minutes for the beans. Drain the vegetables.

Separately hard-boil the eggs, then drain and peel them.

Cut the eggs into small cubes and mix them with the potatoes, carrots and beans. Drain the tuna, flake it and add it to the salad. Then slice the olives, pickles and peppers finely and add them, too. Finally add the mayonnaise and mix it all, taking care not to break up the potatoes.

Normally this is served covered with even more mayonnaise and with a few strips of red pepper on top.

Two-minute mayonnaise

If you are making *ensaladilla*, you had better learn to make a quick home-made mayonnaise, too.

Now that I've spent years observing how grand people live, I've learned that the ultimate grand person's food, found on all the most upper-class tables, is not caviar, truffles, virgin olive oil or fancy cheese. No, it is… Hellmann's mayonnaise. Oh yeah.

But for those of you (and me!) who still prefer home-made mayo – and remember that it was first invented in Mahón, a beautiful town in Menorca – this is an easy way to make it. You can try variations of this sauce: add mustard (though my children prefer it without); half a crushed garlic clove gives alioli, which goes well with fish or rice; 1 tbsp tomato sauce, a few drops of Tabasco and 2 tbsp of orange juice makes a cocktail sauce to be eaten with cucumber sticks or prawns; or add very finely chopped cornichons, capers and herbs to make a tartare sauce to be eaten with fish.

Whichever version you make, you will need a hand-held blender and a tall beaker.

Makes about 250ml

1 egg
200ml sunflower oil (you can make it with olive oil but it may taste a little bitter)
pinch of sea salt
1 tbsp white wine vinegar

Put the egg in the tall beaker. Add the oil. Cover the egg with a hand-held blender, making sure the blender head is at the bottom of the beaker, turning it on but without moving the blender for 30 seconds. It really is important that you do not move the blender at all. You will see how a thick ribbony mayonnaise starts appearing at the bottom of the beaker. Start moving the blender up really, *really* slowly. If you do it slowly enough the mayonnaise will never curdle. When the blender is at the top of the beaker you can then move it up and down with no worries. Add the salt and vinegar and blend again (you can now do this fast). Job done.

The key to this recipe is to think nice thoughts as you are making it; if you think of anything or anybody you do not like, you'll end up with a curdled sauce.

Egg-free mayonnaise

Making mayonnaise with milk instead of eggs is a good trick if you want to keep it in the fridge for two or three days, or if you are using it for a picnic on a sunny summer's day. In fact you can even make it if it is not sunny, as the British summer is largely a question of attitude: you dress for summer regardless of the weather... and it suddenly becomes summer!

Makes about 300ml

200ml sunflower oil
100ml whole milk
pinch of sea salt
1 tsp white wine vinegar

Put the sunflower oil and the milk into a tall beaker. Put a hand-held blender into the beaker, making sure the blender head is at the bottom of the beaker, and switch it on. Keep it running for a minute or so without moving it at all. Don't worry if it looks as if the sauce has split. After about a minute, start moving the blender up very slowly. You will see how a thick sauce starts coming up. Once all the oil and milk has mixed together and the blender is at the top of the beaker, add the salt and vinegar to taste (this needs good seasoning) and mix it in.

Fried squid

This can be served as a snack or a starter. Kids (and adults) simply love it. Some people add garlic, parsley or chilli, but in my view this masks the squid flavour. If you are feeling really self-indulgent, get a baguette, put the fried squid inside it and add a dollop of mayonnaise to make the famous *bocata de calamares* from Madrid. I know you are thinking I have just contradicted myself, but I assure you that the bread and mayonnaise enhance the taste of squid, rather than masking it. Try it: seriously good.

Fresh squid is obviously ideal, but frozen squid (already cleaned and cut) also does the trick, though it has less flavour.

Serves 4

olive oil
sea salt
around 400g squid, cut into rings or sticks
breadcrumbs, to dust
juice of 1 lemon

Put a really generous amount of olive oil in a frying pan and heat it until it is almost smoking. Meanwhile, salt the squid, then dust it with breadcrumbs.

Put the squid in the pan, reduce the heat to medium and fry it quickly (only 1–1½ minutes on each side; if you overcook it, the squid will become tough and rubbery). Squeeze a bit of lemon juice on top and serve immediately.

Empanada

When Nick was in government, every Christmas time we used to give a drinks party to thank his security staff. And yes, when people put their lives at risk for you, it is only right that you say thanks. I could tell you seriously shocking stories about how some well-known politicians have dealt and still deal with their security teams. I won't, because I owe to those who have been responsible for Nick's security the same level of discretion that they have themselves applied to me.

I am often asked if having a person with permanent security in the family was a real burden, and whether I am now relieved that we do not have to have security. In truth it was one of the easiest things to deal with in that situation. Don't get me wrong, having people permanently with us as soon as we stepped out of the house, were inside the car, or even when we were on holiday, did change the dynamic of the family, often in imperceptible ways, as it was easy to fall into the trap of playing a role rather than being yourself. But aside from that, I have nothing but praise for the incredible professionals who have been part of Nick's team, many of whom are now friends.

They see it all: your good moments and your bad, your moments of joy, of sadness… and your arguments as well. And they go through it with a wisdom and respect that cannot be easy to achieve.

This is the recipe for *empanada* that I normally prepared for those Christmas drinks. It is a typically Galician dish, a bit laborious but very delicious. It can also be made with cockles, scallops or salted cod instead of tuna.

Makes a baking tray full

For the filling
4 tbsp olive oil
2 large onions, thinly sliced
½ green pepper, thinly sliced
1 bay leaf
2 × 160g cans of tuna, in oil or
    spring water, drained
2 hard-boiled eggs, sliced
4 canned piquillo peppers, sliced
sea salt
2 tsp sherry or red wine vinegar

For the pastry
500g plain flour, plus more to dust
1 tsp sea salt
1 tsp sweet smoked paprika (*pimentón*)
1 glass (about 150ml) of dry white wine
1 glass (about 150ml) of olive oil, plus
    more for the tray
30g unsalted butter
1 egg, lightly beaten

In a deep frying pan, heat the olive oil for the filling. Add the onions, green pepper and bay leaf. Let them fry over a low heat for 20 minutes more or less, until caramelised and translucent. When cooked, discard the bay leaf, drain away the excess oil and reserve it. Flake in the tuna and add the eggs and piquillo peppers. Add the salt and vinegar, fry for two minutes, then set aside.

Continued overleaf…

For the pastry, mix the flour in a bowl with the salt and paprika. Stir in the wine. Then take the reserved cooking oil and add it to more olive oil until you fill one glass (about 150ml). Add the glass of oil to the flour and wine and mix it all well with your hands until the dough does not stick to the bowl (one or two minutes only).

Cut the butter into 10–12 small cubes. Make holes in the dough with your fingers and 'bury' the cubes of butter in them, then knead it a little to bury the cubes of butter further and work them slightly more into the pastry. Cover the bowl with a cloth and let it rest for 20 minutes.

Line a regular-sized baking tray (usually about 30 × 20cm) with baking parchment and paint it with olive oil. Preheat the oven to 200°C/400°F/gas mark 6.

Cut the dough in half. Put one half on a floured surface, roll it out to the size of the tray and use it to line the tray. Make holes over the whole surface with a fork. Put the tuna filling on top. Roll out the other half of the dough and put it on top. Seal the sides with your fingers and make holes with the fork again. Paint it with the beaten egg.

Cook in the oven at for 45–50 minutes, until golden. Cut into squares and eat at room temperature.

Pimientos de Padrón

Pimientos de Padrón are little green peppers that come from the village of Padrón in the beautiful region of Galicia in North West Spain. Luckily, British supermarkets have started selling them. The beauty of these little peppers is that while most of them are mild, one in every dozen or so is hot as hell. This makes them particularly fun when you are sharing them with friends. If you are a *pimientos de Padrón* fan, as I am, you can sort of guess the ones that are hot. So every time I told Nick I would serve *pimientos de Padrón* as a snack before a dinner he would look at me with panic, for fear that I would serve the hot ones to any of my very *favourite* guests…

Serves 6 as a snack

4 tbsp olive oil
400g *pimientos de Padrón* peppers
generous pinch of sea salt

Heat the oil in a frying pan, letting it get very hot. Add the peppers and toss them a few times. Cover and let them cook for two to three minutes, then take the peppers out of the pan and sprinkle them with the salt. Eat immediately.

Garlic prawns *Gambas al ajillo*

You can find *gambas al ajillo* in most tapas bars, either as a *ración* (a larger dish than a tapa, with bread on the side), or on top of toasted baguette slices with a tiny bit of mayonnaise. The best prawns in Spain come from Huelva, where Columbus's ships started their expedition to discover America.

Calling a Spanish person a 'prawn' is a derogatory term (the saying goes something like: 'you are like a prawn, all of you can be put to good use, except for the head'). Using the language of food to refer to people, especially beautiful people, is common in Spain: a good-looking man is a 'cheese' (*está como un queso*), while a pretty girl is a 'bon-bon' or a 'little sweet' (*un bonbón* or *un caramelito*).

Most of this is part of the art of the *piropo*. *Piropos* are compliments that are given to you in the street (normally from men to women, though I am told it now often happens the other way around). The weirdest one I have heard is, 'I would like to be a pneumonia to live in your chest'. Feminists have complained about *piropos* for years, as objectively speaking they are a bit demeaning for women. But wait to be a 48-year-old feminist as I am, and you'll appreciate the value of being shouted a compliment from a stranger in the street!

The best prawns for this are unpeeled, as unpeeled prawns always have more flavour. Even frozen unpeeled prawns work, provided you defrost them first and increase their time in the pan to three minutes.

Serves 4 as part of a spread

2 garlic cloves, very finely chopped
1½ tbsp olive oil
250g raw prawns, ideally in their shells
sea salt
1 tsp lemon juice (optional)

Just fry the garlic in the oil and, when it starts getting a little colour, add the prawns and the salt. It should take just seconds (and a maximum of one minute) for them to turn from grey to coral pink. As soon as they are pink, sprinkle with the lemon juice and serve. Do not add herbs and be careful not to overcook the prawns.

Peppers stuffed with cod

This is made all over Spain, eaten as a tapa or as a starter. The combination of the smokiness of the pepper and the depth of flavour of the cod works really well. I could easily eat lots of these in one go, but since I am Catholic and therefore prone to guilt, the awareness of the calories in the stuffing is enough to stop me.

Piquillo peppers come in jars or cans and should be whole; you can find them in larger supermarkets and online.

To soak the cod, put it in water for 48 hours and change the water three times. If you can't find salt cod, you can also make this recipe with canned tuna, squid, or a combination of prawns and squid. If you make it with squid, you may want to mix the squid ink with the sauce, for a dramatic colour.

Makes about 16

1 onion, finely chopped
1 leek, finely chopped
75ml olive oil, plus 6 tbsp
200g soaked salted cod
   (see recipe introduction),
   cut into small chunks
8 tbsp Tomato sauce (see page 78),
   or good-quality tomato passata

1 heaped tbsp plain flour
250ml whole or semi-skimmed milk
20 canned piquillo peppers
1 bay leaf
1 tsp chopped parsley leaves

Fry the onion and leek in 4 tbsp of the oil over a very low heat until they become translucent (12–15 minutes). Then add the cod and keep frying for another 10 minutes. Add 4 tbsp of the tomato sauce and let it all simmer for five more minutes. Drain this mixture in a colander over a bowl, reserving the cooking liquid. There may not be much liquid, but it is worth doing in any case so that the mixture is not wet.

Prepare a béchamel by heating the flour in 2 more tbsp of the oil, stirring for three minutes. Separately (in the microwave if you wish) warm the milk, then gradually pour it into the flour mixture, stirring, to make a smooth sauce. Keep stirring until the mixture thickens (seven to 10 minutes). Mix the sauce with the cod mixture and let it cool down a bit.

Stuff 16 of the peppers with the sauce; this really is not difficult, but requires a little practice. Put the stuffed peppers in a shallow sauté pan as you are stuffing them.

Separately mix the cod cooking liquid with 4 piquillo peppers (there are normally a couple that break when you are stuffing them, so just use those) and add 4 more tbsp of tomato sauce. Blend it all together, then pour the sauce over the piquillo peppers, add the bay leaf, sprinkle with parsley and put the pan back over a medium heat for five to seven minutes. That is it.

Or you can forget the sauce completely and just dust the peppers in flour, turn them through beaten egg and fry them in olive oil. You can serve these as finger food.

Tiny tortillas with shrimps
Tortillitas de camarones

This is a wonderful tapa from the South of Spain. It is made with *camarones*, which are tiny shrimps so tender that you can even eat the shells, but it is difficult (if not impossible) to find *camarones* in the UK.

Camarón was also the nickname of one of the most famous flamenco singers, Camarón de la Isla, who was thin and pale, just like a *camarón*.

Giving nicknames to people is a national sport throughout rural Spain. In my village we have whole sagas of nicknames for different families: the Lettuces (*Los Lechugos*), the Breakdowns (*Los Averias*), the Little Tomato (*Tomatito*) the Sparks (*Los Chispas*), the Sucking-Dummies (*Los Chupetes*)… A conversation might run concerning 'the grandson of the Lettuce and the niece of the Little Tomato' who is married to the 'Toasted Maize' as if it was a perfectly normal thing. In my case, since my father was the local mayor for more than 20 years, I've always been 'the daughter of the mayor'… and I suspect that, no matter what I do in my life, that is what I will always be.

Enough for 4–6 as part of a spread

90g plain flour
60g chickpea (gram) flour (from larger supermarkets and Middle Eastern shops)
sea salt
2 spring onions, very finely sliced
2 tsp chopped parsley leaves
100g tiny brown shrimps (you can find these in larger supermarkets)
½–1 glass of olive oil (75–150ml), depending on the size of the frying pan

Mix both types of flour in a bowl with the salt, spring onions and parsley. Pour in 300ml of water, stirring well as you do so, to create a mixture without lumps. Then stir in the shrimps.

Heat the olive oil in a frying pan until it is very hot. Pour 1 tbsp of the mixture into the oil to form each *tortillita*, being careful not to overcrowd the pan. Wait until the *tortillita* becomes golden (about 50 seconds), then turn and allow to become golden on the other side, too (only about another 20 seconds). Take them out and put them on kitchen paper to blot off any excess oil, then eat them immediately, while you fry the rest. They are crunchy outside and soft inside, very delicious.

EGGS

My maternal grandmother, María, had many hens and, as a result, we ate eggs pretty much every day when we were staying with her. She would have laughed hard had she lived to witness all the silliness that has been said about limiting one's intake of eggs nowadays; she fed everyone in her family at least three a day!

After seeing an early draft of this book, my editor (who is really brave, as it takes some courage to publish a cookery book written by a lawyer) told me that I was 'strong on eggs'. I have been called many things during the five years of the coalition government, but, I tell you, being 'strong on eggs' is something I could have never have predicted would be said about me. Unfortunately I made the rookie mistake of telling this to my kids, and now they have made it a regular way in which to tease me. When they see me losing my patience, their response is often, 'Don't worry mum, at least you are strong on eggs!'

Crispy fried egg

I do realise that this isn't really a recipe, but it deserves its place in this book nonetheless. These have nothing in common with the limply fried eggs that some restaurants serve. They contain a considerable amount of olive oil, which strengthens the flavour.

To make a fried egg crispy, just fry it in truly hot (almost smoking) oil. García Lorca, a very famous Spanish writer (*The House of Bernarda Alba* is his most famous play in the UK, but you should really read the poem 'Lament for the Death of Ignacio Sánchez Mejías', or the play *Yerma*) used to call these 'eggs with lace' (*huevos fritos con puntilla*). He used to eat them at a B&B in Tordesillas where he was for a while, a very beautiful town close to my village beside the river Duero.

These are great on their own with lots of baguette-type bread. You can also eat them with a bit of Ibérico ham on the side, or simply with fries. My paternal grandmother sometimes added ¼ tsp of paprika to a couple of tbsp of the frying oil (while the pan was still on the heat) and, after 15 seconds, she added 1 tbsp of red wine vinegar.

Makes 1

5 tbsp olive oil
1 egg
pinch of sea salt

Put the oil in a small frying pan, heat it until it gets smoky, then crack the egg into the oil, add salt, get a spoon and pour some of the hot oil on top of the egg. It should take barely 30 seconds (though it depends on how runny you like the yolk). Eat it immediately.

Stewed eggs

These were often made by my maternal grandmother, María.

Normally for dinner she would give us a couple of fried eggs, but if she was feeling cheerful, she would make stewed eggs. Frankly the eggs themselves are no better than fried eggs, but the sauce – that sauce with lots of bread – was a good enough reason on its own for us to try to get my grandmother into a good mood...

Serves 2

2 tbsp olive oil
1 garlic clove, finely chopped
¼ onion, finely chopped
1 tbsp plain flour
½ glass of white wine (about 75ml)
1½ tsp finely chopped parsley leaves
1 bay leaf
4 eggs
sea salt

Pour the oil into a frying pan and place over a medium heat. Add the garlic and onion and fry until they become translucent (seven minutes, more or less). Add the flour, stir for 30 seconds, then pour in the wine with about three-quarters of a glass (110ml) of water. Throw in the parsley and the bay leaf.

Once the sauce is bubbling, reduce the heat, wait for four to five minutes, then carefully crack in the eggs, one by one. Sprinkle with salt, cover the pan and let the eggs stew for three or four minutes, depending on how you like them. Discard the bay leaf and eat immediately with lots of bread.

Tortilla de patatas

My village is a place with 3,500 inhabitants where families have been living together for decades. We simply know everything about each other. My father was mayor for almost 20 years and my mother taught at the secondary school for four generations, so there is absolutely no way for us to go unnoticed. Thus, when people ask me whether I find the British media intrusive, I often smile, because honestly the gossip in my village makes the British tabloids look like rank amateurs! Most of the gossip happens over a snack, and one of the most typical snacks throughout Spain is a *pincho de tortilla* (a bit of *tortilla de patatas* with bread on the side).

Against that background, the attempts by Nick's security team to pass unnoticed in my village were always going to be a fiasco. The first time they sent a policeman from the Met – 'discreetly', they said – they sent him dressed in tweeds (in the middle of Castile... yep, discreet!). I was in London, but as soon as he arrived, I received a call from the receptionist at the local hotel whispering, 'There's a secret policeman here, what should we do with him?'

The poor thing did not speak a word of Spanish so he could not easily find his way about. I must have received at least 10 emails from people in the village about what 'the secret policeman' was doing during the day. This concluded when the head of the local police decided to simply invite him for lunch and be open about the fact that the whole village knew who he was. The incident gave my village gossip for at least a week.

There are as many recipes for this as there are Spaniards: some like it with onion, some leeks; some prefer it 'blonde', some 'dark'; some 'runny', some 'dry'... try it a few times and find the version that you prefer. My advice: do not add chorizo, or peppers; be generous with the salt; and you need a good non-stick frying pan and very hot oil.

Serves 6 as a snack, or 4 for lunch

500g potatoes	lots of olive oil
1 onion, finely chopped	5 eggs
sea salt	

Chop the potatoes into really thin slices, by hand or with a food processor. Mix the onion and the potatoes and add salt. Put a really generous amount of olive oil in a large frying pan over a medium heat, add the potatoes and onions, reduce the heat to its minimum, cover with a lid and fry until all is golden, tender and soft (more or less 20 minutes). Put them in a colander placed over a bowl to get rid of the excess oil (reserve this oil).

Beat the eggs. Add the potato mixture to the eggs with a tiny bit more salt.

Return three spoonfuls of oil from the potatoes to the pan and place over a high heat until it is very hot. Add the egg mixture and reduce the heat to medium-low. Once you see bubbles on the surface (10-ish minutes), turn the tortilla. This seems more difficult than it is. You can do it by flipping it on to a big plate (I do it over the sink just in case some of the mixture falls off). Slide back into the pan and let the tortilla cook on the other side; another eight minutes, more or less. Eat hot or at room temperature.

Salt cod omelette

I love salted cod. If any of the guys running British supermarkets would like to make me really happy (there is no reason they should, but it's worth a try, just in case), they would start selling two new products: salted cod and fresh Spanish cheese. I am convinced that both would be a hit.

Salted cod has a subtle, complex flavour that takes what is already a really nice fish to a totally different dimension. I even like it raw with a few black olives and vinaigrette, but this very simple omelette is one of the best ways to cook it.

To soak the cod, put it in water for 48 hours and change the water three times.

Serves 2 for lunch, or 4 as part of a spread

3 tbsp olive oil
3 spring onions, finely chopped
½ green pepper, finely chopped
200g soaked salted cod (see recipe introduction), cut into small chunks
4 eggs

Heat the olive oil in a frying pan over a gentle heat and fry the spring onions and green pepper. As soon as the spring onions are translucent and the pepper is soft (five to 10 minutes), add the cod and let it all fry for three or four minutes so that the cod breaks into small flakes. Tip the contents of the frying pan into a colander placed over a bowl, to remove the excess oil (reserve this).

Beat the eggs, then add the cod mixture and mix well.

Wipe out the frying pan. Add the reserved olive oil to the pan, with a little more if needed, and get it as hot as possible. Pour the eggy mixture into the pan and reduce the heat to medium. After a couple of minutes, turn the tortilla by flipping it over a big dish, then slide it back into the pan to fry on the other side. We do not add any salt to this, but you may want to add some to the mixture before you fry the omelette.

Baked eggs

My grandmother on my father's side, Angela, used to prepare this dish when we went to visit her on Sundays. She cooked the eggs slowly on the open wood-burning stove (the authentic version of the Aga) that was usual in rural Spain until democracy brought cooking with gas to our homes.

My grandma measured scarcely 1.38m, but she managed to give birth to eight really tall sons. So when people ask me whether, having three sons, I would like to try for a daughter, I just think of my grandmother…

All the quantities here are purely indicative, so add more or less to taste.

Serves 1

1 tsp olive oil
1 tsp grated onion
10–15g chorizo, cut into cubes
10g Serrano ham (ideally), or bacon, cut into cubes
handful of frozen peas

3 tbsp Tomato sauce (see page 78), or good-quality tomato passata
1 egg
sea salt and, if you wish, freshly ground black pepper

Preheat the oven to 180°C/350°F/gas mark 4.

Heat the oil and grated onion in a saucepan over a medium heat until the onion becomes golden. Then add the chorizo and ham or bacon and fry for two minutes. Add the peas and, after three or four minutes (or seven minutes if the peas are still frozen), the tomato sauce. Let it bubble for one minute.

Take it off the heat and put it in an ovenproof dish or ramekin. Crack the egg on top. Add salt (and pepper, if you want) and bake for 12–14 minutes until just set.

Peasant's tortilla

This is a really nice tortilla that my mother makes sometimes for dinner when she cannot think of anything else. It is meant to be the classic dish made with leftover 'little bits of everything' that Spanish peasants would normally eat, though the recipe must have evolved over the years, as peasants were unlikely to have had leftover canned tuna lying around...

Serves 4

50g chorizo, finely chopped
50g Serrano or Parma ham, finely chopped
100g peas (frozen are fine here)
6 eggs
50g canned tuna, in oil or spring water, drained
5 canned piquillo peppers, finely sliced
sea salt
olive oil, enough to cover the base of the pan

Place a frying pan over a low heat and fry the chorizo and ham for three or four minutes (you don't need any oil). Then add the peas and let them get soft for another three or four minutes (if they are still frozen, this may take as long as seven minutes).

Separately beat the eggs well. Add the tuna, peppers, chorizo, ham and peas to the eggs with a pinch of salt (remember the chorizo and ham are salty, so don't overdo it).

Pour the oil into a non-stick frying pan. When it is very hot, add the eggy mixture. Let it fry for three minutes, then reduce the heat and continue to cook for another four minutes. Turn the tortilla by flipping it over a big dish, then slide it back into the pan to fry on the other side for three or four minutes. Eat it immediately.

Iberian scrambled eggs

I spent five years saying 'I can only speak about what *we* do,' every time I was asked whether I thought it was OK that politicians used their children in pictures. But the real answer is a common sense: 'Of course not!' One just has to look around to realise that, helpful as it may be for the politician at any given time, it is just too big a risk for the kids, both from a security and a mental sanity point of view. If you only knew how much choreography goes on behind any of the political pictures that are presented as 'natural', you would conclude in no time at all how very wrong it is to get your children in those pictures.

During the last general election I was watching the news with one of my sons, when I saw a film of one of the leaders making scrambled eggs while his children were approaching the camera and playing with it. I exclaimed, 'Oh my God, look at those children!' just as my son exclaimed, 'Oh my God, look at those scrambled eggs!' My son definitely has the upper hand when it comes to the priorities in life…

The key to any really good scrambled eggs (whether in this recipe, or the plain and unembellished version) is to do the 'stir, lift and fold' movement which is the key to avoiding miserable-looking scrambled eggs. This is how you make a happy-looking pan of scrambled eggs.

Serves 1

3 canned piquillo peppers, cut into strips, plus 1 tbsp of the can juice
1 tsp olive oil
2 slices of Serrano or Parma ham (the ham will be slightly fried, so no need to get an expensive one)
1 tsp chopped parsley leaves
2 eggs
pinch of sea salt (not too much as the ham is salty anyway)

Heat a non-stick frying pan over a medium heat. Add the piquillo peppers with the 1 tbsp of their liquid. When the liquid has evaporated (one or two minutes), remove them from the pan.

Heat the olive oil in the pan, tear the ham slices into strips and add them to the pan with half the parsley. Wait for one minute, then return the peppers to the pan.

Lightly beat the eggs, add the salt and pour them into the pan. Stir with a wooden spoon, using a 'stir, lift and fold' movement. After a couple of minutes they are done. Just sprinkle the rest of the parsley on top and eat immediately.

Chorizo omelette

This is always a winner with kids. It is even better when served with plenty of crusty bread and a very cold beer (not for the kids, of course!).

It is a very simple lunch for children beginning to cook for themselves. Learning to make an omelette is a basic skill. Frankly there is no mystery to it, so they will learn fast. It is best if they practise with plain omelettes first (which in Spain are called 'French omelettes'. Not sure why).

Once they master this basic skill they can add ham, mushrooms, grated cheese, parsley or chives… Chorizo omelette is a very Spanish choice, though my own favourite is with tuna; if it was up to me that would be my dinner every day: a tuna omelette and a salad. But put this chorizo omelette in a sandwich – made with a baguette and eaten while still hot – divine!

Feeds 2 children or 1 adult

100g chorizo, thinly sliced or in small cubes
olive oil
2 eggs
small pinch of sea salt (be careful, as chorizo is salty anyway)

Heat a frying pan (without oil) over a low heat. Fry the chorizo for 1–1½ minutes (it will release a lot of red fat). Put the chorizo on kitchen paper and throw away the fat. Wipe out the pan.

Add enough olive oil to the pan to coat the base very thinly and heat it until it is very hot (this is the trick to all omelettes, so that they do not stick to the pan). Lightly beat the eggs, add the chorizo and the salt and tip it all into the oiled pan. Reduce the heat and flip the omelette when the underside is golden. (The easiest way is to put a plate on top of the frying pan, turn it over, then slide the omelette back into the pan to cook on the other side.) When it is golden on both sides (this takes a couple of minutes), take it out and eat it.

SALADS
AND
VEGETABLES

As a general rule, Spanish vegetable dishes are served before a main meal, expected to be eaten on their own rather than relegated to side dishes, as is often the case in the UK.

Vegetable side dishes became a surprisingly important task for me when I became the wife of one of the leaders of the coalition. I was expected to spend hours designing menus, talking about flowers for the dinner table and having pointless conversations about things that – honestly – nobody in this century should care about. I have often wondered what would have happened if, instead of wives, the leaders of the parties had husbands. I suppose, in that case, all these tasks would be allocated to the politician's personal assistant… and I bet my neck that would be a woman as well!

As far as I was concerned, I reached saturation point the day I was on a business trip making a trade legal assessment in one of the remotest parts of Africa. I happened to be in a mine on top of a massive dragline and surrounded by people. Though coverage there is rather patchy, my mobile phone kept ringing insistently. When I finally answered, it was the office in Chevening 'urgently' wanting to know… 'What kind of vegetables *exactly* would you like for the dinner on Saturday night?' I think my answer was something like, 'Green, any green vegetables,' though probably inside I was thinking, 'The f***ing vegetables kind!!'

The dishes here should not get you in such a state…

Tomato sauce

This is a basic. A kitchen (or freezer) without tomato sauce is like a garden without flowers, or a village without a pub. Having a good tomato sauce at hand means you have half your dinner ready. There are endless dishes – many of them in this book – you can prepare with this: pasta with tomato and chorizo, pasta with tomato, cod with tomato and peppers, meatballs, tuna with tomato, chicken with tomato, fried eggs with tomato, white rice with tomato, lasagne, peas with tomato, beans with tomato... you name it. It is so good that you can also eat it on top of bread, or simply with a spoon.

In Spain it is a bit pointless to try to teach this recipe to children as, when they leave home, their Spanish mothers (mine included) keep bringing Tupperwares full of home-made tomato sauce to their offspring. That is if they leave their homes in the first place of course, which now happens much less often than you might think...

You can prepare three or four kilos of tomatoes at the same time and freeze most of the sauce. It keeps for a couple of months in the freezer, or a week or so in the fridge.

You will need a hand food mill (this is also very useful for vegetable purées, mashed potatoes and baby food). You can buy them inexpensively.

Makes about 1.5kg

olive oil
2kg tomatoes, fresh or canned (in winter it is better to use canned tomatoes)
1 green pepper
1 red pepper
3 onions
3 garlic cloves
1 bay leaf
sea salt and freshly ground black pepper
1 tsp caster sugar (optional)

Coat the base of a large pan generously with olive oil and place over a medium-high heat. While the oil is heating, cut all the vegetables into large chunks. Once the oil is hot, add all the other ingredients except the sugar. Let it fry for 10–15 minutes, then reduce the heat to its lowest setting and let it bubble for 1–1¼ hours. (If you are using a pressure cooker you only need 25 minutes, but you will need to evaporate off some of the cooking liquid.)

Remove the bay leaf and process all the mixture through the hand food mill. Taste it and adjust the seasoning. If you let it bubble for the indicated time, the sauce should not be acidic. However, if you think it is not sweet enough, you may choose to stir in the sugar (or even better, add a carrot next time you prepare it).

Children normally like getting the sauce through the mill, but beware, because your kitchen may end up looking like a battlefield afterwards.

Beans with *ajoarriero*

Ajoarriero is a very Castilian sauce. We use it with beans, cauliflower and cabbage, but also with salted cod, and you can pour it over fried eggs as well. It comes from the sauce that the shepherds – who transported sheep from one region to another during the winter – used to prepare their meals. The regular transport of sheep by foot in Spain stopped many decades ago, but even today you can see the main street in Madrid (the Castellana) taken over by sheep once every year.

Serves 4–6 as a side dish

sea salt
600g runner beans, cut into small chunks
2 carrots, finely chopped
1 potato, cut into small chunks
2 tbsp olive oil
2 garlic cloves, finely sliced
1 tsp sweet smoked paprika (*pimentón*)
1½ tbsp red wine vinegar

Set up a large saucepan or steamer of salted water. Boil or steam the beans, carrots and potato for 15 minutes, or until soft, not al dente. When they are ready, drain the vegetables.

Meanwhile, heat the oil in a frying pan over a medium heat, fry the garlic until lightly golden (be careful not to burn it or it will taste bitter), add the paprika, stir for five seconds, then pour in the vinegar all in one go (be careful because it will spit). Add 3 tbsp of water, then take it off the heat.

Add the sauce to the bean mixture in a saucepan and let it cook over the heat for two or three minutes, so all the flavours mix well.

Romesco sauce with roast leeks

This is typical of Catalonia. It is normally eaten with young onions, called *calçots*, but leeks make a good substitute and, anyway, romesco is a wonderful sauce that can be served with many dishes, from rice to grilled fish or meat. I like the smokiness of this sauce so much that I could easily eat it with a spoon. The flavour of *pimentón* is very strong, so you need only a tiny pinch.

Serves 4 as a starter or light lunch with bread

3 tomatoes
1 onion
1 head of garlic
½ glass (about 75ml) of olive oil, plus more for the vegetables
8 leeks
sea salt
10 almonds
1 tbsp red wine vinegar
slice of coarse country bread (preferably stale)
pinch of sweet smoked paprika (*pimentón*)

Preheat the oven to 200°C/400°F/gas mark 6. Cut the tomatoes and onion in half and put them on a baking tray, add the head of garlic and a little oil and roast it all for 35–40 minutes. When this is ready, squeeze the garlic paste out of the garlic head and discard the skins. Put into a food processor with the tomatoes and onion.

Meanwhile, clean the leeks well. Seal them in foil, two at a time, with a little salt and oil. Heat a griddle pan and put the foil packets on top for five minutes on each side, turning once. Put the packets in a roasting tray and roast beside the vegetables for the sauce for 20–25 minutes. (Be careful when you open up the foil, especially if children are helping, as very hot steam will come out.)

Toast the almonds in a dry frying pan for a couple of minutes. Then add 1 tbsp of the oil to the frying pan, pour the vinegar over the bread and fry the bread in the oil on both sides (less than one minute on each side). Add the bread, almonds and paprika to the food processor with the remaining oil and half a glass of water (about 75ml) and blend until smooth.

Let the leeks cool down a little and serve them with the romesco sauce.

Chickpea salad

This is a very simple summer salad with two of the most traditional Spanish flavours: chickpeas and chorizo (and it is 'co-ree-tho' not 'cho-reeso', or 'chorit-zo').

It does not look too pretty, but it tastes amazing. It comes from the South of Spain and originally did not contain feta cheese. My – extremely stubborn and slightly food chauvinistic – Spanish family still refuse to eat it with feta and believe I have adulterated a good Spanish dish but, honestly, the cheese works really well with it.

Serves 4 as a side dish or as part of a spread

400g jar or can of chickpeas, drained and rinsed
3 spring onions, finely sliced
100g feta cheese, cut into small squares
150g chorizo, cut into small squares
1 garlic clove
½ tbsp red wine vinegar or sherry vinegar
1 tbsp olive oil
1 tbsp chopped parsley leaves

Mix the chickpeas, spring onions and feta cheese. Place in a salad bowl.

Dry-fry the chorizo cubes lightly, then add to the salad, discarding the oil that runs out of the chorizo. Grate the garlic and mix it in a small bowl with the vinegar and olive oil. Mix this dressing well with the salad. Sprinkle the parsley on top. We do not add any salt, as the feta is naturally salty, but add some if you wish.

Aubergines with honey

After the European election in 2014 (a particularly low point), I decided to get the family to Granada for my birthday. If you have not been there, the city is well worth visiting: spectacular and full of history.

As we arrived there to have dinner with one of my friends, we witnessed one of the biggest storms I have ever seen in my life. Litres of water poured from the sky, to the point that the main square in Granada looked like a swimming pool and you literally had to take off your shoes to be able to walk through it.

We sought refuge at random in one of the restaurants beside the square and, as we were getting installed at the table, one of my sons came back with news: 'there is a Roman soldier in the loo!' The security team went to check and confirmed that he was correct: there was indeed a guy dressed as an ancient Roman in the loo.

As soon as we sat down, and to the amazement of the security team, there appeared not one, but more than 40 guys dressed as Roman soldiers and women in Roman tunics toting guitars. It turned out that one of the carnival groups of Cádiz was performing at a theatre nearby and had decided to come in for a bite.

In one of the most surreal nights of the five coalition years, we (and that included the security team) ended up clapping to rumbas played by a group of Roman soldiers and singing with them the '*tri-qui-ti-tran-tran-tran*'… (You don't know the '*tri-qui-ti-tran*'? Honestly, it is time for you to catch up!)

This is a very typical dish from Granada, that children love (and it is a really good way to get them to eat aubergines).

Serves 4 as a snack or starter

1 aubergine
small bottle of fizzy water or beer
    (don't worry, the alcohol evaporates)
sea salt
75g plain flour

25g chickpea (gram) flour (if you do not
    have this then use plain flour, but the
    aubergines won't be as crispy)
1 glass of olive oil (about 150ml)
3 tbsp honey

Cut the aubergine into thick matchsticks, put in a bowl and cover with the fizzy water or beer. Let them rest for 30 minutes.

Drain the aubergine sticks and salt them well. Then combine the flours in another bowl. Heat the oil in a frying pan until it is very hot (this really has to be very hot, so whenever you think it is ready, give it a couple more minutes). Dust the aubergine sticks with the flour and fry until golden on both sides (do not fry too many at a time, or the temperature of the oil will reduce and the aubergines will not become crispy). They should turn golden after a minute or so on each side. Remove from the pan with a slotted spoon and drain on kitchen paper while you fry the next batch.

Heat the honey with 1 tbsp of water in a small pan for 30 seconds. Pour it over the aubergines. That's it.

Chard with ham

Chard is a very underrated vegetable. My uncle produces tonnes of it during the summer and, because he knows I like it, he keeps bringing kilos to us when we are on holiday in Spain. This is one of the recipes you can make with it. Don't use too much salt, as chard is a naturally salty vegetable.

Serves 4 as a side dish

1kg chard (it reduces a lot in volume when it cooks)
2 tbsp olive oil
3 garlic cloves, very finely chopped
50–75g Serrano or Parma ham, finely chopped, to taste
sea salt
1 tbsp red wine vinegar

Cut the chard stalks and leaves into slices. Steam the stalks for five minutes.

Heat the oil in a frying pan, add the garlic and cook for a couple of minutes until it turns golden. Then add the ham, cook for another minute and finally add the steamed chard stalks and the chard leaves. Add the salt and sprinkle with the vinegar. Let it simmer for five minutes, turning to wilt the leaves, and it is done.

Roast peppers and roast tomatoes

Roast peppers are a fantastic summery dish. They really are the taste of the Mediterranean sun, regardless whether you eat them in sunny Spain or in the more unpredictable British summer. Delicious with grilled meat or tuna, fried eggs, or just with bread... and if that was not enough, they are also full of vitamin C.

It takes a while for children to get used to this flavour, but teaching children to roast vegetables is a very easy thing to do and it is a good way to show them how much flavours can change between raw and roast.

PEPPERS

Preheat the oven to 200°C/400°F/gas mark 6. Get six big peppers, the bigger the better. Put the peppers in a roasting tin and add a bit of water (half a glass, or about 75ml more or less). Put the tray into the oven and roast the peppers for 35 minutes. Then turn them and roast them for another 30 minutes. They should come up rather black.

Let them cool down, then peel them (this is easier if you put them into a plastic bag as they are cooling down). Add 3 tbsp of the liquid that the peppers have produced while roasting, 3 tbsp olive oil, 1½ tbsp good sherry vinegar (though they are also nice with balsamic vinegar) and salt.

You can keep these for a few days in the fridge, or even freeze them, provided you do not add the oil or vinegar.

TOMATOES

Preheat the oven to 200°C/400°F/gas mark 6. Cover a roasting tin with cherry tomatoes. Add sea salt, a little olive oil, 2–3 squashed garlic cloves and, if you wish, a few basil leaves. Toss it all well with your hands or, if you do not like the smell of garlic, with a spoon. Roast for 40 minutes or until they start to get black around the edges. Eat with meat, cod, omelettes, on their own, on toast, with a salad...

You can roast regular tomatoes in the same way if you cut them into quarters (give them 15 more minutes in the oven), but children tend to prefer cherry tomatoes simply because of their dinky size.

Courgette 'pasta' with prawns

I am not generally keen on food fashions, but there is a lot to be said about the craze for spiralling vegetables, as children seem to find it an interesting way to eat them. If you want to give it a go and you are, like me, prone to buying useless gadgets, avoid the temptation to purchase any of the expensive spiralising tools that are now on the market. The likelihood is that they will end up at the back of a cupboard with the huge bread-making machine that you bought thinking that the smell of fresh bread in the morning would miraculously make your life more wholesome, and the ice cream machine that you bought under the dream of a never-ending sunny summer… while living in the rainy UK. Instead, a hand-held spiraliser cutter that works like a pencil sharpener is relatively cheap and easy for teenagers to handle and does the job well. I have a Zoodle, but Lakeland sell a version, too.

We make this with courgettes, as they are provided in huge quantities by another uncle when we are in Spain in the summer. Courgette plants are very prolific and we always end up with more than we can possibly eat, even after sharing the daily harvest with the neighbours. A couple of years ago a Japanese doctor wrote a best-seller about healthy food in which he rubbished courgettes. I am going to spare you the expletives from my uncle when he heard this…

Serves 4

3 tbsp olive oil
1 leek, finely chopped
3 courgettes
2 garlic cloves, sliced

200g raw prawns, peeled and deveined
juice of ½ lemon
handful of parsley leaves

Heat 2 tbsp of the oil in a large saucepan over a medium heat. Reduce the heat, add the leek and let it fry until soft. Cut the courgettes into ribbons (you do this by twisting them in the Zoodle cutter as if you are sharpening a pencil, it only takes a minute per courgette more or less). Add the courgettes to the pan, increase the heat and let them fry for 10 minutes.

In a separate frying pan over a medium heat, add the remaining 1 tbsp of oil and fry the garlic for a minute until golden. Add the prawns and let them fry for five minutes. Right at the end add the lemon juice and parsley, let the sauce bubble for 30 seconds, then add it all to the courgettes.

Toss it together as you would any pasta dish and serve.

Vinagreta

This is a Spanish 'sauce-that-is-almost-a-salad'. It is fun for children to make as you can do it all in a food processor. You can have it with prawns, green salad, cucumbers, steamed leeks, boiled potatoes, radishes, boiled eggs or (small) pasta. I like this (and all things vinegary) so much that I can easily eat a whole bowl of it on its own.

Serves 6 (or 1 if you eat it, like me, with a spoon)

½ mild-flavoured onion
1 red pepper
½ green pepper
½ garlic clove
½ tbsp chopped parsley leaves
1 hard-boiled egg
plenty of olive oil
sea salt
white or red wine vinegar, to taste

Roughly chop all the vegetables and herbs, tumble them into a food processor and chop finely. Finely chop the hard-boiled egg white and stir it in by hand. Mash the egg yolk into a little olive oil. Stir this into the vegetables, then stir in 2–3 tbsp more olive oil, until it starts to look a bit like a sauce. Add the salt and vinegar and serve.

Carrot salad

One of the best ways to get children to eat carrots is grated in a salad.

My farmer uncles complain often that people do not eat enough carrots, which keeps their price for farmers too cheap. As a result, in our family we eat so many carrots that our effect on demand must single-handedly increase the price some weeks.

You can replace the sesame and coriander with pine nuts and parsley, if you prefer.

If children help you to make this, they like using graters, but supervise them closely as they can cut themselves easily. Also, be careful when you toast the sesame seeds, as some of them can pop out of the frying pan as they are toasting.

Serves 4 as a side dish

1 tbsp sesame seeds
coriander leaves, to taste
4 carrots, coarsely grated
2 tbsp olive oil
sea salt
1 tbsp red wine vinegar

Toast the sesame seeds in a dry frying pan over a medium-low heat, watching them all the time as they burn very easily. Add the seeds and the coriander to the carrots in a bowl. In another smaller bowl, mix the olive oil, salt and vinegar and add it to the salad. Toss and serve.

Fresh produce at a market in Asturias

Easy Mediterranean salad

Though Spain produces wonderful vegetables, we do not seem to have a huge variety of salads. In fact, if you ask for a salad (*ensalada*) in any Spanish restaurant, what you get is lettuce, tomatoes and cucumbers with an olive oil and red wine vinegar dressing. My British friends also find it rather peculiar that we never make a proper vinaigrette: we just pour the oil and vinegar directly over the salad. I agree, it is a bit weird, but it's a great way to cut down on preparation time!

This easy Mediterranean salad is really simple to make and a good way for kids to start getting used to dressing, as the bread will cut the acidity of the vinegar. In Spain the saying for salads is, 'salty, oily and not very vinegary,' but, at the end of the day, this has to be made to taste. The rule in my home, though, is never to add sugar to a dressing. If you are tempted to do that, then have a dessert instead.

For some weird reason my children only eat salad if they prepare it, so I always ask them to mix the ingredients and add the dressing. They can do this on their own... but (and this applies in particular if they are boys) remind them to wash all the vegetables first!

Serves 4 as a side dish or as part of a spread

1 pitta bread
2 tomatoes, chopped
1 cucumber, chopped
2 tbsp olive oil
1 tbsp white wine vinegar
sea salt

Put the pitta bread in a toaster so it becomes crunchy. Tear it into small pieces.
Now all you need to do is to mix all the ingredients and serve.

Winter salad

If you come to our house in the winter for a dinner party, you are likely to eat a winter salad (which is handy, because it means the first course is ready before the guests sit down). This is a combination that works particularly well, partly because it mixes sweet and acidic flavours as well as cold and warm components. It also looks very pretty, which is a bonus when you have guests. Use spinach or rocket instead of salad leaves, if you like, or a mixture.

Serves 4 as a starter

200g skinned and deseeded butternut squash, cut into strips
2 tbsp well-flavoured olive oil, plus more for the squash
sea salt
50g diced bacon, or Serrano ham
handful of pine nuts
1 tbsp balsamic vinegar
packet of salad (young leaves are best)
100g goat's cheese

Preheat the oven to 200°C/400°F/gas mark 6. Put the butternut squash on a tray, coat it with olive oil and salt and roast for 20 minutes (the edges should be brown).

Fry the bacon or ham in a dry frying pan for five minutes. Remove with a slotted spoon and place on kitchen paper to blot off the excess fat. Toast the pine nuts in the same pan (be very careful because they burn easily, they just need around one minute).

Mix the 2 tbsp of olive oil, the balsamic vinegar and a little more salt.

Assemble the salad: mix the vinaigrette with the leaves and place in a salad bowl. Put the bacon on top, then the roasted squash, crumble the goat's cheese over and finally scatter with the pine nuts to serve.

Mushrooms

Though I make mushrooms often on winter weekends, my children rejected them for years. The first time I proposed cooking mushrooms together with them, I had hoped that by actually preparing them they would be inclined to at least taste them. It was a complete failure: they hardly touched the mushrooms when they were cooked and had developed a darker colour; one of my sons tried just a tiny piece; another said he wanted to vomit just from looking at them...

They kept refusing to taste them again until, recently, one of my sons declared out of the blue that he loves mushrooms... and then the others simply followed suit. Peer pressure seems to be the trick...

Serves 4 as a starter or a side dish

2 tbsp olive oil, plus more to serve (optional)
50g bacon, cut in little cubes
250g mushrooms, sliced, but not too thinly
1 garlic clove, crushed
1 tsp finely chopped parsley leaves
1 tbsp red wine vinegar
sea salt and freshly ground black pepper

Heat the olive oil in a sauté pan over a medium heat. When the oil is hot, add the bacon, reduce the heat and wait until the bacon is golden (three or four minutes). Increase the heat and immediately add the mushrooms, garlic, parsley and vinegar. Wait for five to seven minutes until the mushrooms are darker but develop a nice gloss, then add the salt and pepper (if you add the salt any earlier the mushrooms will get too watery) and serve.

You may want to add a little bit more olive oil on top (just a few drops), to make them even glossier.

Quick potatoes

If you need something quick to accompany a meat dish, this is what you can do. Easy peasy for kids. And the smell of the oregano lends a touch of the Med.

Serves 4–6 as a side dish

2–3 potatoes, cut into small cubes
sea salt
1½ tbsp olive oil
1 tsp dried oregano

Mix all the ingredients well with your hands so that all the potatoes are coated in the oil and flavourings. Put them on a microwaveable dish, cover it with cling film ensuring there are no gaps (or just put them in a microwave bag), and microwave on a high setting (I use a 700W oven) for 4½ minutes.

By this time they should be soft, otherwise get them back in the microwave for another couple of minutes. Be careful when you are removing the cling film from the dish, particularly if you are doing this with children, as really hot steam will come out.

Then heat a pan (without any oil), put the potatoes in and let them fry for one or two minutes until they get a bit of a colour.

Easy.

Self-important potatoes
Patatas a la importancia

My mother cooks this dish to perfection. The recipe comes from the Tierra de Campos, where she was born, and it was a way to fill the stomachs of a large family with something delicious at very little cost.

Talking about my mother and a recipe in the same sentence is a bit absurd. Her cooking instructions tend to run something like this: 'fry it until you think it is OK'; 'leave it simmering for a while'; 'put some water in'; or 'add as much flour as it takes'. This is truly inexplicable, because when it comes to science experiments (she was the chemistry and physics teacher at my school), her instructions are precise to the nanomillimetre… but, like most good cooks, when it comes to food, the only way to get her recipes is to cook with her and observe what she does.

This was one of my father's favourite dishes; he loved hearty food. The key to making the humble potato taste this good is in the sauce.

Serves 4 as a side dish

sea salt
2 big potatoes, cut in 1cm slices
plain flour, to dust, plus 1 tbsp
1 egg, lightly beaten
plenty of olive oil
½ onion, finely chopped
3 garlic cloves, finely chopped
1 bay leaf
2 tbsp chopped parsley leaves
1 glass of white wine (about 150ml)
pinch of saffron threads

Salt the potato slices. Put some flour on a plate and the egg in a dish. Dust the potato slices with flour and then turn them in the egg on both sides. Heat the olive oil in a frying pan over a medium heat and fry the slices on both sides until golden (four minutes on each side, more or less). Put them on kitchen paper to blot off the excess oil and then transfer them to a shallow sauté pan.

Put 4 tbsp of the frying oil into a saucepan. Heat the oil, then reduce the heat. Fry the onion gently for four minutes, then add the garlic and bay leaf. When the onion and garlic are translucent (after eight minutes or so), add the parsley. Add the 1 tbsp of flour and let it fry for two minutes. Then increase the heat and pour in the glass of white wine, 500ml of water and the saffron. After the saffron dissolves (30 seconds, more or less), add a bit more salt and pour the sauce over the potatoes.

At this point you can set aside the dish to reheat later, or carry on now. Put the pan over a medium heat and let it simmer for 30 minutes, then serve.

Peas with tomato sauce

The transition to democracy in Spain brought with it 'modernity'. In my village, this meant that my father, as mayor, was able to cover the streets with cement, as opposed to the muddy earth paths that we had endured up until then. He was also able to repair all the almost-fallen-down churches and to bring in new factories: a sugar factory that was built by Polish workers and was our first encounter with other European nationalities; and a frozen food factory, which meant that all the farmers in the village started growing peas.

At a more down-to-earth level, modernity brought many changes to our lives, such as colour TV, Tupperware… and bikinis. I mean this seriously: since all communications were censored, Swedish tourists wearing bikinis on Spanish beaches in the early 1970s was a determining factor in the transition to democracy, as it meant that Spanish people – who had to cover up to their necks – could see first-hand how 'free' people outside Spain were.

Modernity also had its downsides. In my village the new openness meant that, for the very first time, we got a brothel. The problem was not just that it existed, but rather that it was set up very close to the village, so it was easy for many men to sneak out there in the evenings 'for a drink'. My father, who was a saint, used to receive complaint after complaint from the wives in the village. He decided to do some gentle digging… and discovered that the brothel was ultimately owned by a priest!

This is a recipe that you can make with peas. Yes, frozen peas.

Serves 4–6 as a side dish

3 tbsp olive oil
¼ onion, finely chopped
¼ green pepper, finely chopped
1 garlic clove, finely chopped
80g chorizo, or Serrano or Parma ham, cut into little cubes
500g frozen peas
sea salt
1 bay leaf
4 tbsp Tomato sauce (see page 78), or good-quality tomato passata
½ tsp balsamic vinegar

Heat the oil in a frying pan. Add the onion, green pepper and garlic and let it fry over a medium heat for eight minutes. Add the chorizo or ham and fry for three or four minutes. Then add the peas, salt and bay leaf and keep cooking it all for 15 minutes.

Add the tomato sauce, then the balsamic vinegar. Increase the heat for four or five minutes, then serve.

Nick and I during the 2015 general election campaign

At Chevening, preparing for an event with an outdoor meal

Nick and I at the 2014 Party conference

The cooking behind the politics

The kitchen has always had a role in politics: the group of advisers to a politician are traditionally called a 'kitchen cabinet' and, when politicians invite others to dinner, the biggest honour is to be invited to the politician's kitchen table. The kitchen is important not only to the politician, but also to their families: if the politician is a man, as happens in my family, the media often likes to portray the wife as a traditional woman whose territory is the kitchen… no matter what she actually does in real life.

If you think I am exaggerating, let me share this with you: during the 2015 general election, two TV channels asked to interview the leaders of the parties and their wives in their kitchens in order to assemble a 'personal portrait' of them and their families. I agreed to one of them on the condition that they would not film our children and that they would also interview me in my office about a campaign I was leading with female role models and girls. They did spend an hour in my office recording the interview, but when the programme was broadcast, they did not use a single second of that interview, not even a passing image; every single shot of me was in the kitchen. Apparently, picturing wives of politicians working in an office is a stretch too far.

I couldn't care less whether women choose to play traditional roles and spend their lives in kitchens. That is up to them (and I spend a lot of time in the kitchen myself!). But I definitely do not want girls to grow up being told that they have to fit the old-fashioned image of women ruling in the kitchen… while men rule the world.

In my own family, where my husband Nick and I share pretty much everything, the kitchen is nevertheless my territory; Nick has many talents, but I am sure that even he would agree that cooking is not among them.

If something worries or bugs me and I do not find the answer in my mind, I always go for one of two formulas: I either cook, or go for a run. In fact, I normally cook first and then – out of guilt because of all those calories – go for a run. If my family gets to the kitchen and I have prepared a complicated dish, their immediate question is always, 'Are you OK?'

Just as cooking and food has kept me close to my Spanish roots, family and friends, it has also carried me through the world of politics. I have cooked lots during the coalition years, truly lots: I have cooked and stirred thinking about what Nick being in politics would mean to our children; I have chopped and bashed thinking what I would tell some politicians and journalists if I had the chance; I have kneaded and proved trying to find the patience required to keep my mouth shut; and I have prepared endless meals for us to share with friends, advisers, colleagues, party members and supporters.

Nick cooking – a rare sight!

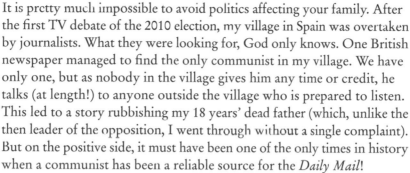

It is pretty much impossible to avoid politics affecting your family. After the first TV debate of the 2010 election, my village in Spain was overtaken by journalists. What they were looking for, God only knows. One British newspaper managed to find the only communist in my village. We have only one, but as nobody in the village gives him any time or credit, he talks (at length!) to anyone outside the village who is prepared to listen. This led to a story rubbishing my 18 years' dead father (which, unlike the then leader of the opposition, I went through without a single complaint). But on the positive side, it must have been one of the only times in history when a communist has been a reliable source for the *Daily Mail*!

Apart from that, my family and friends had fun keeping the media on its toes: when the tabloids sent journalists to remote villages where my cousins and second cousins live, they pretended they were unrelated to me; they sent them to speak to people I had never met and directed them to neighbouring villages where I had never been. It became a 'trick the foreigner' game, as only Spanish people can play…

The differences between Spanish and UK politics have been fascinating to watch from the front line. How the public mood in this country changes with regards to political parties and individuals is, in all honesty, one of the things that I still have not mastered. From Cleggmania to burning effigies of Nick… it was a step-change that was hard to digest. But, then, you find yourself losing an election and the level of public warmth sharply climbs up. Going out with Nick nowadays means talking to endless people who approach him to offer sympathy and respect (not to mention all those who want selfies!). It is simply impossible to get that kind of mature reaction in the highly tribal world of Spanish politics. So yes, that is one of the things that makes me a bit jealous of politics in the UK… just one of the many things…

In exchange for all that turmoil I have been given the chance to be a front-row spectator to a truly interesting period of British politics. I would not have changed that for anything. I have learned an enormous amount, not only about politics, but about human nature, too. I have seen good and bad, met some of the best people I know and also some of the worst. And I have witnessed some amusing moments, as well. Politics is a serious business but, like most other things in life, it is at its best with a pinch of humour.

Food for entertaining

These are some of the menus that I have used often for the many – so very many! – meals that I have prepared at home during the coalition years:

Winter salad (*see page 99*)

–

My grandma's Stewed lamb
(*see page 156*)

–

Pineapple and mint salad
(*see page 242*)

Pimientos de Padrón and
Garlic prawns (*see pages 55 and 57*)

–

Marmitako (*see page 117*)

–

Lemon posset with Cat's tongues
(*see pages 237 and 261*)

Salmorejo (*see page 39*)

–

Roast fish with potatoes
(*see page 136*)

–

Poshed-up yogurt
(*see page 250*)

Fish soup (*see page 22*)

–

Chicken with apple
(*see page 144*)

–

Cheese with *Membrillo*
(*see page 229*)

Roast fish (see page 136)

FISH

Fish is one of the most versatile foods there is. It is a pity that there is not more (and a greater variety of) fish served in an island like the UK… the reason being, of course, that most British fish is exported elsewhere (a lot of it to Spain). One just has to visit Dorset or Cornwall (or the stunning Norfolk) to see how wonderful the fish is there.

Spanish people love fish. Especially fish with bones, such as conger, and we adore whole roast fish, head and all, as keeping a fish intact increases the succulence of a dish. It takes a while to get used to cooking and serving a whole fish with bones, but once you do you will see that it takes the experience of eating fish to a totally different level.

If you have the chance to show children a proper fishmonger's shop or stall, do, so that they learn to recognise fresh whole fish. Ask them to look at the eye and see whether it is transparent (cloudy eyes are a bad sign), and also to check that the gulls are properly vibrant red (dull brownish gills betray fish that has been out of the water for too long). I am afraid that when we buy filleted fish – which in the UK we do all the time as there is nothing else available in most supermarkets – we just do not know what we are paying for.

My home country is known internationally for over-fishing, a reputation that I am not sure is fair. Some years ago, during the fish war between Canada and Spain, the *Financial Times* published a wonderful article in which, after enumerating all the legal arguments in favour of each of the parties in the International Court of Justice dispute, they rightly concluded that, at the end of the day, fish should be 'for those who know how to eat it'. Knowing how to eat fish is one of the things we Spaniards do very well.

Sailor's clams *Almejas a la marinera*

Good clams are difficult to find (and also expensive), so it is a pity to ruin them with a creamy sauce, such as in chowder. This sauce is subtle and not too thick. The key to this dish is, of course, the quality of the clams; a good clam should taste of the sea and it is one of the most exquisite types of seafood there is. If you cannot get good clams, don't even try to cook this. And, equally, if you do not appreciate seafood, don't waste your money on clams.

Many Spanish people eat this dish at Christmas or New Year's Eve; it really isn't everyday food. New Year's Eve is normally spent with family, and people go out until really late. At midnight, Spanish people eat 12 grapes with the 12 dongs of one of the main clocks in Madrid. If by this time you have managed to get through the whole Christmas period without having the mother of all fights with your family, then you can declare that – for another year – you and your family are all doing well.

Serves 4

500g clams, well scrubbed and soaked in salted water (see page 22)
1 onion, very finely chopped
olive oil
½ glass of white wine (about 75ml)
juice of ½ lemon
1 tbsp fine breadcrumbs
1 tbsp very finely chopped parsley leaves
1 bay leaf
sea salt (not too much as clams are naturally salty)

You are meant to cook the sauce first and then place the clams on it to steam open. However, if you are, like me, paranoid about rotten seafood, do this first: heat a pan until it is rather hot. Put the drained clams in it with 2 tbsp of water, cover and wait for a couple of minutes until they open up. Discard those that remain closed. Do not throw away the liquid at the bottom of the pan; strain it through a sieve and set aside.

In a different pan, fry the onion very slowly in a little olive oil until it gets soft and a little bit golden. Increase the heat and add the wine. Wait while it bubbles away, then add the lemon juice, 1½ glasses (about 225ml) of water, the liquid from the clams, the breadcrumbs, parsley and bay leaf (and the salt if you think it is needed). Let it all boil for four to five minutes. The sauce should not be acidic. If it is (this can depend on the quality of the wine), just add more water.

When you are about to eat, heat the sauce until you see bubbles coming up, add the clams and take them off the heat after just one or two minutes (otherwise they will turn rubbery). Serve straight away with plenty of bread.

Marmitako

This is a very typical dish from the fishing villages in the North of Spain. The name refers to it being cooked in a casserole (*marmita* in Spanish).

My mother prepares this every summer when we are many for lunch and tuna is in season. I think the secret of her recipe is that she cooks the vegetables and the tuna separately so that they fry, rather than boil. She also uses a generous amount of good Spanish wine.

Marmitako is 'conversation food'; if you have *marmitako* for lunch, you should stay talking over the table for a good while after the meal, not least because it is on the heavy side, so it is good to digest it with time. It is either that or a good summery siesta, which is healthy as well. In any case, *marmitako* is really food to share. The children love this dish. As for the adults, it is imperative that you drink it with a glass of very cold Albariño (a white wine from Galicia; there are lots of good versions in British supermarkets) or Rueda (a white wine from Valladolid, where I come from).

There is a lot of controversy over tuna so, when you buy it, check that it is responsibly sourced. It is, like all fish, not cheap, but two steaks go a long way in this dish.

If children are helping to make this or any other fish dish, you need to be strict about them washing their hands after touching the fish, or they might end up with food poisoning.

Serves 5

4 tbsp olive oil, plus more for the potatoes
2 thick tuna steaks
sea salt
2–3 tbsp plain flour
1 large onion, cut into thin half moons
¼ green pepper and ½ red pepper, finely sliced
½ tomato, finely chopped, or, even better,
   2 tbsp Tomato sauce (see page 78)
1 bay leaf
1 garlic clove
handful of chopped parsley leaves, plus more to serve
1 glass of white wine (about 150ml)
5 potatoes, cut into medium-sized chunks

Heat the 4 tbsp of oil in a large sauté pan over a medium heat. While the oil is heating up, cut the tuna steaks into chunks, salt them and dust them with the flour. Fry them for one to two minutes on each side, then set aside.

In the same oil, fry the onion and peppers (and fresh tomato if you are using it), reducing the heat so that they get soft and sweet (10–15 minutes). When they are ready, return the fish to the pan. Add the bay leaf and the tomato sauce (if you are using it).

Continued overleaf...

Grind the garlic clove with half the parsley in a mortar and pestle, mix in the wine, then pour the contents of the mortar into the pan. Add a glass (about 150ml) of water, wait until there are bubbles in the sauce and let it simmer over a low heat for around 10 minutes (it is really difficult to overcook this dish, so do not worry too much about precise timing). You can keep the fish stew for one day in the fridge and it actually tastes nicer the following day as the sauce thickens.

When you are ready to eat, salt the potatoes and separately fry them in olive oil until golden but not completely soft (this takes four to five minutes). Put them on kitchen paper to blot off the oil. Meanwhile, reheat the *marmitako*, if necessary, for 10 minutes over a medium heat, then add the potatoes. Cover and wait for another eight to 10 minutes until the potatoes are soft and the whole dish mellows. Add the remaining parsley (this is not necessary to the flavour, but the dish looks nicer).

Casa Pilatos, a very beautiful house in Seville

Squid in its ink *Calamares en su tinta*

My brother, who has been into good food ever since he was weaned, is crazy about this recipe. When he was little he used to order in restaurants: 'calamares as a starter, calamares as a main dish and calamares for dessert'. And even though he is now in his 40s, he continues to love them.

Ask the fishmonger to give you the squid ink: it comes inside a kind of whitish bag, like a little sausage. If you cannot get it, some fishmongers sell small plastic sachets of artificial ink which tastes very good too (and makes the dish even darker).

Try this with plain rice. Or with lots of bread.

Serves 4 as part of a spread

2 tbsp olive oil
500g squid, cleaned and cut into
    bite-sized pieces
8 tbsp Tomato sauce (see page 78),
    or good-quality tomato passata

1 garlic clove
handful of parsley leaves
½ glass of white wine (about 75ml)
the ink of each squid (or see recipe
    introduction)

Put the oil in a sauté pan. Add the squid and let them fry over a high heat for four to five minutes. They will release some water, so wait until it all evaporates. Add the tomato sauce. Crush the garlic with the parsley in a mortar and pestle, stir in the wine and 75ml of water and pour it over the squid. Do not add salt; squid are naturally salty.

Now, put the ink sacs into a small sieve over the pan, pour a bit of hot water on them and mash with the back of a spoon so that the ink falls into the squid pan. (Or just add the contents of the sachets.) Let it all simmer for 15 minutes over a low heat.

This dish keeps well for a couple of days in the fridge and it is probably better the day after you make it.

Hake in green sauce *Merluza en salsa verde*

Hake is The Fish in Spain. You can find it in every Spanish fishmonger. Good hake is flaky and has a subtle taste. It can be hard to find it in British supermarkets, but you can get it at fishmongers (and, of course, online) and its price is more or less the same as that of haddock.

Generally speaking, fish is cheaper in Spain than in the UK, but even families that struggle economically eat fish: they may be cheaper varieties, but they still appear on the table once or twice a week.

This dish comes from the North, but it is typical all over Spain. The key is not to overcook it (the same goes for any fish really). You can use hake fillets, but it is better (and more authentic) with thick slices of bone-in hake.

Serves 4

3 tbsp olive oil
1 onion, finely chopped
2 garlic cloves, finely chopped
1 tbsp plain flour
1 glass of white wine (about 150ml)
½ handful of chopped parsley leaves
1 bay leaf
sea salt
4 portions of hake, ideally on the bone
handful of clams, well scrubbed and soaked in salted water (see page 22)

Put the olive oil in a sauté pan over a low heat and fry the onion and garlic for 10 minutes. Add the flour and mix well for a minute or so. Add the wine. Stir for a minute and then add the chopped parsley, bay leaf and a little bit of salt. Then add 150ml of water and let it bubble for two or three minutes. Finally salt the fish on both sides and add it to the pan. Let it all simmer for five minutes (do not turn the hake or it will break up).

Meanwhile, heat a frying pan and add the drained clams (discard any that have cracked shells, or that are open and refuse to shut when sharply tapped on the sink). In less than a minute they will open up (discard any clams that do not open). Add the clams to the pan with the fish. Strain their cooking juices through a sieve and add those, too.

You can also cook the sauce in advance, refrigerate, then reheat it and cook the fish in it just before you are going to eat.

Basque cod

This recipe was given to me and my mum decades ago by a Basque fishmonger from Medina del Campo. Medina is a market town very close to my village. It is there that Isabel I of Spain (the Catholic Queen) died. And, ever since the Middle Ages, the town has held a Sunday market that sells the most wonderful produce, including great fish.

If you do not have home-made tomato sauce you can replace it with good-quality shop-bought tomato passata. We use canned peppers, preferably the Spanish piquillo variety that are widely available in supermarkets, though Italian canned roasted peppers are good, too. But if you are serving this to children and they find the taste of piquillo peppers too strong, just leave them out.

Serves 4

2 garlic cloves, finely sliced
olive oil
sea salt
4 x 120–130g cod steaks
plain flour, to dust
10 tbsp Tomato sauce (see page 78), or good-quality tomato passata
100ml white wine
4 canned piquillo peppers
chopped parsley leaves, to serve

Slice the garlic and fry it for one minute in the olive oil (do not let it get too golden). Set aside. Salt the cod steaks, dust them with flour and fry for two minutes on each side over a medium heat in the same oil in which you fried the garlic. Add the tomato sauce and then the white wine. Put a pepper on top of each fish steak and sprinkle it with a bit of the garlic. Sprinkle a bit of chopped parsley on top and let it simmer over a low heat for five minutes to burn off the alcohol in the wine. That is all.

Salmon en papillote

Looking good for politics is not a task to be undertaken lightly. Indeed, it is often a full-time job, which explains why many wives of politicians around the world quit their own careers. You are meant to look beautiful but not too beautiful, modern but not too modern, a nice adornment to your husband but always to avoid becoming centre stage. You think that is absurd? You are right!

Your passport to freedom comes when one of the 'women's interest' magazines praises you for your fashion sense and declares you have style. This happened to me at the Royal Wedding. From that moment onwards, you are just fine: you wear something that does not match? Something ugly? Or perhaps even ridiculous…? No worries, it is because you have 'style'.

The pinnacle of the looking-good achievement is to look 'effortlessly chic'. If you are one of those women (or worse, one of those girls) who worry about this, let me reassure you – and I say this from bitter experience – that looking chic requires not just an effort, but a monumental one: dyeing your hair, brushing it, taking care of your skin, doing a 'natural' make-up yourself (or getting somebody to do it for you), judging your wardrobe carefully, spending hours at the gym. And then, when you have achieved all that, look at yourself in the mirror and turn it down a notch… yes, again! Ladies, 'effortlessly chic' simply does not exist! So, wear something that makes you feel good and forget about what anybody else may say.

Eating lots of salmon gives a glow to your skin. Completely imperceptible of course… but you already know that!

Serves 1

1 tbsp olive oil	½ courgette
sea salt	finely grated zest and juice of
1 salmon steak	½ unwaxed lemon
½ carrot	splash of white wine
½ leek	

Preheat the oven to 200°C/400°F/gas mark 6.

Take a big rectangle of aluminium foil, or baking parchment. Put the oil on top. Salt the fish and put it on the olive oil. Cut the carrot, leek and courgette into thin batons and put them on the salmon. Add the lemon zest and juice and the wine. Make a packet or bag with the foil or parchment, making sure that there is room for air to circulate inside the bag and that it is sealed well all the way round so that air cannot get out. If you are not sure that it is properly closed, put the packet on another large piece of foil and seal that, too. Put the packet in the oven and bake for 10–12 minutes.

You can also make this with halibut or cod, in which case replace the carrot with some sliced tomatoes, which work better.

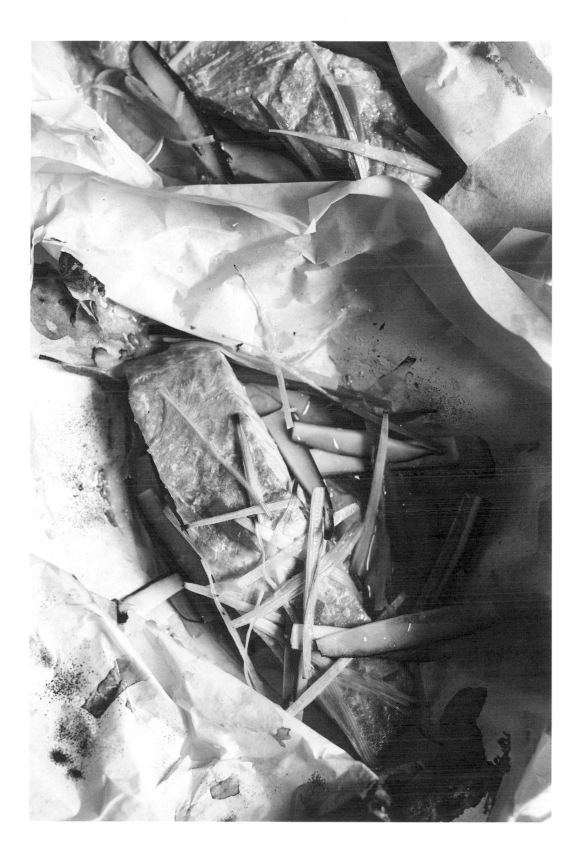

Tuna with tomato sauce

This is a good way to prepare tuna, as you can feed many people with just a few steaks. My grandmother used to cook it in July when the Spanish wheat is ripe, when tuna is in season, so that she could feed all the family and friends who came to help my grandfather with the harvest.

Serves 6

2–3 tbsp olive oil
3 tuna steaks, each 120–130g
sea salt
4 tbsp plain flour
1 large egg, lightly beaten

10 tbsp Tomato sauce (see page 78)
1 bay leaf
1 garlic clove
¾ glass of white wine (about 110ml)
handful of parsley leaves

Pour the olive oil into a sauté pan over a medium heat. Cut the tuna on the diagonal until you get about six thin slices from each steak. If the slices are very small you can hammer them a bit with a glass or a cup so they become bigger and thinner. Salt them. Put the flour and egg in two dishes, salt them, and coat the tuna first with flour and then with the egg. Fry them for a couple of minutes on each side until they become golden; you may need to do this in batches if the slices won't all fit easily in the pan.

Add the tomato sauce and the bay leaf to the pan with all the tuna and heat it all for three or four minutes. Separately crush the garlic in a mortar and pestle. Stir in the wine, then pour the contents of the mortar into the tuna and tomato pan. Simmer for a minute or so, then add half a glass of water (about 75ml) and the parsley and let it bubble for five to seven minutes, so some of the sauce evaporates and the flavours mix.

This dish is better if you prepare it the day before you are going to eat it.

Salmon in *pepitoria*

Another recipe from my grandmother's family, this time perfected by my mum. Very easy, very tasty, yet rather delicate.

My grandma used to make this with conger (which was always full of bones) as, at the time, salmon was simply unaffordable. She could never have imagined that salmon would actually become cheaper than conger or even sardines.

Personally I agree that conger is a better fish for this, but it *is* full of bones. Salmon is therefore the safer choice. As always, the better the fish the better the flavour... but if you actually get hold of really fresh wild salmon, then just grill it or roast it and eat it without any sauce. And if you do not like salmon, you can try this recipe with monkfish instead.

Serves 4

2 eggs	1 bay leaf
2 tbsp olive oil	4 skinless salmon steaks
1 garlic clove	sea salt
½ glass of white wine (about 75ml)	1 tsp chopped parsley leaves

Boil the eggs for 10 minutes. Peel them and separate the yolks from the whites. Chop the egg whites finely (the easiest way is to mash them with a fork) and set aside.

In a sauté pan, mix the oil with the egg yolks, again mashing them with a fork. Put the pan over a medium heat. Crush the garlic in a mortar and pestle, mix it with the wine and add it to the pan. When you see bubbles (after a minute more or less), add a glass of water (about 150ml) and the bay leaf.

Sprinkle the salmon steaks with salt and put them into the sauce. Let them simmer for three or four minutes for fish that is still moist in the middle (if you like the salmon well done, leave it in for another two or three minutes). You may need to add a bit more salt to the sauce. Right at the end, discard the bay leaf and sprinkle the fish with the parsley and chopped egg white.

Salpicón

Though we are in the 21st century, one of the things that is still required of any woman close to politics is that she 'dresses up for the show'.

The UK media is one of the best things in the country and some individual British journalists are some of the most intelligent and accomplished people I have ever met. But when it comes to women, the story goes like this: if you are the wife of a Tory leader, the interest of the Conservative media to defend you as an asset is so overwhelmingly strong that no matter how you look, what you say or do not say, what you do or do not do, they will protect you at all costs. But if you are the wife of one of the other leaders, you are on your own. This is because, when the Conservative media attacks you (and they will do that no matter what, precisely because their overwhelming interest is to destroy any sources of power that disrupt their cosy relationship with the Conservatives), the more progressive (and therefore disorganised, and often rather self-righteous as well) media will simply not come to your defence.

So, what do you do? It is simple: you protect yourself by dressing up well! In that way all critical articles will have a few paragraphs about how lovely you look, or a particularly good photo of you. In the world of politics that means crisis aborted… and all is well.

If I'd had more emotional strength I would have simply realised that these attacks are never personal and refused to play the game. But I only found that strength halfway through, when it was too late.

This Spanish recipe is a 'looking pretty' dish… and it is very healthy, so I'm sure that has an effect on how good you will look as well!

Serves 4–6

400g monkfish
sea salt
10 raw or ready-cooked prawns
½ onion (red onion if you like a milder flavour), finely chopped
1 tomato, deseeded and finely chopped
3 hard-boiled eggs
4 tbsp olive oil
1 tsp mayonnaise (for home-made, see page 49)
1 tbsp white wine vinegar
pinch of chopped parsley leaves

Simmer the monkfish in salted water for 10 minutes, then drain the water and let it cool down. Briefly poach the prawns in boiling water for a couple of minutes if you are using them raw (devein these), but this is good with shop-bought cooked prawns, too (don't poach those). Cut the monkfish and prawns into bite-sized chunks and place in a bowl.

Add the onion and tomato. Then chop two of the eggs and the egg white of the third egg and add to the bowl. Separately mix the oil and the third egg yolk in a small bowl, mashing them with a fork, then add the mayonnaise and finally the vinegar. Mix with the fish and sprinkle with the parsley. This is best eaten at room temperature.

At the Royal Wedding

Fried hake

In Spain this recipe is called '*merluza a la romana*' (in the Roman style) and it is cooked in a thin (not crunchy nor heavy) batter, which means that the predominant taste is of the fish, not of the batter. If you want an even lighter (but very good) version of this, coat the fish only in beaten egg and forget about the flour completely. The recipe works well with cod, too.

Serves 4

plenty of olive oil
plain flour, to dust
1 egg, lightly beaten with 2 tbsp milk
sea salt
4 x 1–2cm thick slices of hake

Heat the oil over a high heat in a small frying pan. Put the flour in a dish and the egg and milk in another.

Salt the fish and dust it in the flour on all sides. Shake it to get rid of the excess flour. Coat it in the egg and milk mixture, then fry it for a couple of minutes on each side or until golden, reducing the heat to medium once you put the fish in the pan.

Fish is better under- than over-cooked, but if the slices of fish are quite thick and you are concerned that children may be put off by slightly underdone fish, put them into a microwave on a high setting – I use a 700W oven – for 20 seconds (no more).

*Fish at a market in Asturias,
one of my favourite places in Spain*

LUBINA DE
MAR

Tuna salad

At Party conferences I lived on salads. The Party conference is meant to be, absurdly, The Moment for the leader's wife… and was often a real headache to me. It is a kind of cross between a wedding and an exam: you walk hand-in-hand with your husband in front of the media and then you wait for the verdict (in writing) from them.

Not even Nobel prize winners have to be kissed in public by their partners after their once-in-a-lifetime acceptance speeches, so I'm not sure why it is felt necessary for politicians and their spouses to do so after (yet another) political speech. When the Party advisers complained in various years that I did not go to the podium for a kiss and a round of applause, my answer was, 'I only receive applause on a podium when I deliver the speech myself.' To their credit, they didn't even try to find any arguments to counter this.

Much as I would like to think that what I did or did not do depended on me, the truth is that I (a woman) was only able to resist this and other tiny humiliations that happened regularly at conference because Nick (a man) stood firmly behind me.

Serves 1

any type of lettuce, shredded
  if necessary (optional)
5 canned piquillo peppers,
  cut into strips
160g can of tuna, drained and flaked

handful of black olives
3 tbsp olive oil
1 tbsp balsamic vinegar
½ tsp mayonnaise (for home-made,
  see page 49)

Just arrange the lettuce (if using), peppers, tuna and olives in layers. In a small bowl, whisk the oil, vinegar and mayonnaise. Pour this vinaigrette over the salad and eat. If you like some crunch, you can add a couple of slices of raw onion on top.

At the Party conference, spring 2015

Lemon sole

This is a very versatile recipe that you can prepare with various types of fish (try it with haddock). You can cook it in minutes and it is very easy for children to learn. It is also very easy to remove the bones of sole. Mine love this dish: butter and lemon juice, what's not to like?

The amount of fish may seem too much for a child, but mine devour it every time; and yes, it is not cheap, but it is after all very good fish.

Serves 5

5 lemon sole fillets
50g unsalted butter
sea salt
plain flour, to dust
handful of parsley leaves
juice of 1½ lemons

Wash the fish and pat it dry with kitchen paper. Melt half the butter in a large sauté pan. While the butter melts, salt the fish, dust it with the flour and shake it a bit to get rid of any excess flour.

Fry the fish, skin side down, for two or three minutes, then flip it over and fry it again for a couple of minutes. Remove from the pan.

Add the remaining butter to the pan. Once the butter melts, add the parsley, let it fry for 30 seconds, then add the lemon juice. The parsley splutters a lot, so be careful. If you are scared of the spluttering, add the lemon juice to the butter first and then add the parsley (it will be less crispy, but very nice anyway). Pour the sauce over the fish.

Salmon en croute

This is a really good way to make salmon interesting for children. Mine have come to hate salmon, after eating it once every week, to the point that they have decided to go on a collective 'salmon strike'… yet they still agree to eat this.

Serves 4

2 leeks, finely chopped
1 tbsp olive oil, plus more for the tray
1 tbsp unsalted butter
a few spinach leaves
1 tbsp crème fraîche
sea salt and freshly ground black pepper
1 sheet of ready-rolled puff pastry
350g salmon (2 thick fillets), skinned
1 egg, lightly beaten

In a pan, fry the leeks over a medium-low heat in the oil and butter for 15 minutes. Add the spinach leaves and toss it all well. After one more minute, add the crème fraîche, salt and pepper, wait until it bubbles, then take it off the heat. Preheat the oven to 200°C/400°F/gas mark 6.

Unfurl the puff pastry and salt and pepper the salmon. Put the salmon in the centre of the puff pastry and spoon the leek mixture on top. Wrap it all with the pastry, encasing the salmon well. Press the edges of the pastry together with a fork so that the seams do not open up. Put it seam-side down on an oiled oven tray (it must be oiled, so that it does not stick).

Paint the pastry with the egg. Bake for 25–30 minutes, until golden.

Roast fish

During the five years of the coalition, the Prime Minister, his wife, Nick and I met together only on three occasions: three dinners, two at their place and one at ours. It might-perhaps-be-possibly-most-likely-in-some-probability my own fault that we did not meet more often, as I refused invitation after invitation to get the families together at Chequers (a place that, to this day, I have not visited), but work is work… and friends are friends.

I am afraid that at the dinner at our kitchen I made a serious faux pas. I had bought a wonderful whole wild fish and I roasted it. The flavour was simply amazing, but I forgot that most English people are not used to eating fish with bones… there were compliments all round on the recipe, but it was definitely not a pretty scene!

Roast fish is one of the two best ways to eat a good whole white fish (the other is to roast it covered with salt). The main thing is not to cook it for too long; fish is expensive, so don't ruin it by overcooking.

Serves 2–4, depending on the size of the fish

4 potatoes, cut into slices as thick as a £1 coin
1 tomato, peeled and cut into thick slices
1 onion, thinly sliced
3 tbsp olive oil
sea salt
1 whole fish, ideally with head on
1 glass of white wine (about 150ml)
juice of 1 lemon
handful of chopped parsley leaves

Preheat the oven to 220°C/425°F/gas mark 7.

Put the potatoes, tomato and onion in a roasting tin. Add the olive oil and a bit of salt and let this roast for 25 minutes. Then salt the fish inside and out and put it on top of the potatoes. Add the wine and lemon juice along with a glass (about 150ml) of water, sprinkle the parsley on top and roast for about 20 minutes. It is impossible to give precise timings for this as it depends on the thickness of the fish. You can see whether it is properly cooked by making an incision with a knife in the thickest part; when the flesh is white and opaque (not translucent), it is done.

Merluza a la gallega

This is a wonderful dish from Galicia. They have some of the best fish in Spain and as a result the main principle of Galician cuisine is to do as little as possible to the fish, in the knowledge that even the best sauce will always taste worse than a truly fresh, succulent piece of hake. You really should only try this dish with round slices of hake cut through the whole fish; I know it sounds odd, but boneless fillets just don't taste the same here.

Many people know Galicia because it is the region where the stunning Santiago de Compostela, a world-renowned pilgrimage site, is based. If you are Catholic and you manage to walk the 200km of the 'Camino de Santiago' (St James's Way) you will be forgiven for all your sins… just by walking, fancy that! Going to Galicia to eat *merluza a la gallega* will not achieve such levels of forgiveness for you, but it is certainly well worth the trip.

Children can help with it all (and like to pour the reddish oil over the fish), but be careful if they help to take the fish out of the pan, as it can easily break.

Serves 4

4 bay leaves
sea salt
1 onion, halved
4 big potatoes, peeled and halved
4 thick round slices of truly fresh hake on the bone
5 tbsp good olive oil
2 tbsp sweet smoked paprika (*pimentón*)

Pour two litres of water into a large saucepan and bring it to the boil with the bay leaves, salt and the halved onion. Add the potatoes, reduce the heat and simmer for 10–15 minutes until almost tender.

Salt the fish slices on both sides, put the fish in the pan, reduce the heat and cook for five minutes, ensuring the water does not boil (if you see any bubbles in the water take the pan off the heat; I know this sounds petty, but if the water boils the fish will dry out and you will have wasted your time and money…). After five minutes, take the pan off the heat and wait for another five minutes.

Carefully remove the fish and potatoes from the water with a slotted spoon and put them on a plate (discard the bay leaves). Mix the oil and paprika with 1 tbsp of the cooking liquid and pour it over the fish and potatoes. This is one of the best ways to eat hake.

Mackerel pâté

'Blue' fish (the romantic Spanish term for that type of fish usually called the far-less-attractive 'oily fish' in the UK) are the sancta sanctorum of healthiness. If you buy them smoked they are quite high in salt, but even in that way, I think mackerel is still a good thing for children to eat. I like fresh mackerel dusted in flour, fried with a couple of sliced garlic cloves and 2 tbsp of vinegar, with half a glass of water (about 75ml) added to the pan. But the recipe below ('that fishy thing' as it is disrespectfully called in our home) is the only way to get my children to eat mackerel. They never seem to get enough of this.

Serves 4–6 as a snack or starter

4 fillets of smoked peppered mackerel, skinned
200g crème fraîche or double cream
juice of 1 lemon, or 1½ lemons if you like strong flavours
1–1½ tsp horseradish sauce, to taste
a little smoked sweet paprika (*pimentón*, optional)

Put all the ingredients except the paprika in a blender or food processor. Blitz them well. Chill in the fridge for five to 10 minutes. Serve as it is, or sprinkled with paprika.

My children like making this (or anything that involves a blender). They complain forever about the smell that is left on their hands, though…

Quick grilled fish

This is a really fast – and also very healthy – dinner. My children happen to love fish, but even if yours are not too into it, they will normally be more inclined to taste food if they have helped to prepare it. You have a choice of two ways to prepare the fish here; the second takes longer, as you need to bake the sliced potatoes first.

Serves 4–6

With onion and lemon
olive oil
sea salt
4–6 fillets of white fish
1 onion, finely chopped
2 lemons, 1 cut into thin half moons
1 tbsp chopped parsley leaves
½ glass of white wine (about 75ml)

On a bed of potato and tomato
olive oil
3 potatoes, thickly sliced
2 tomatoes, thickly sliced
sea salt
4–6 fillets of white fish
1 tbsp chopped parsley leaves

To make the fish with onion and lemon, preheat the grill to its maximum temperature. Cover the bottom of a roasting tin with a bit of olive oil. Salt the fish and put the fillets in the tin. Sprinkle the onion on top with the sliced lemon and parsley. Add a bit more olive oil, then the juice of the other lemon, then the wine.

Put the roasting tin in the oven for 10 minutes (check after seven minutes as the temperature of grills varies a lot). The fish is ready when the flesh is white and opaque, not translucent.

Mine like to eat plain grilled fish with rice, but it is nice with potatoes, too.

To prepare the fish on a bed of potato and tomato, preheat the oven to 220°C/425°F/gas mark 7. Cover the bottom of a roasting tin with a bit of olive oil. Layer on the potato and tomato slices, then drizzle with more oil. Bake for 20 minutes.

Now preheat the grill to its maximum temperature. Salt the fish and put the fillets on top of the potatoes. Sprinkle with parsley. Put the roasting tin in the oven and grill for 10 minutes, as above.

MEAT

When I was growing up, it was easy to trace where the meat we ate came from because it was normally from my village and, if we were with my grandparents, from the backyard. My grandmother María was a master at killing chickens – by wringing their necks – and rabbits, by giving them a sharp knock on their head. She got a bit carried away at times: I swear I found her once trying to kill moles (they drove her berserk as they destroyed all her veggies) by pouring water into all the holes but one and waiting for the mole to emerge from that final hole so she could hit it with a stick. An authentic version of whack-a-mole. Luckily, moles are fast animals – faster than my grandma – so they survived.

My paternal grandmother would kill a pig each autumn, using every part of it to make chorizo, lomo, stews, hams… true 'nose-to-tail' eating. This was quite a celebration and even the children of the family would be present at the dispatch of the beast.

Nowadays it is much harder – and far more expensive – to get good meat. As a general rule, though, buy what you can afford. Eating meat less often is better for health anyway. And some cuts, such as cheeks or minced meat, are much cheaper than the more prestigious joints but still taste superb.

Chicken with apple

This is a regular when we have friends for dinner, mostly because it tastes better the day after you cook it, so it actually makes sense to prepare it in advance.

For my grandma, María, this recipe used to start by going to the orchard or the barn to pick up some apples, then going to the farmyard, killing a chicken with her own hands (she could be seriously vicious… but hopefully that is not genetic), then plucking it. Sometimes when I give speeches about the fact that women have an unfair deal, a picture of my grandmother killing a chicken comes to mind. Women have really come a long, long way… at least as far as chickens are concerned…

Serves 4

2–3 tbsp olive oil
sea salt
6 chicken thighs, or 1 chicken cut into 8
1½ onions, chopped into half moon slices
½ red pepper, finely chopped
2 garlic cloves, finely sliced
3 carrots, finely chopped
2 tbsp sherry vinegar
1 bay leaf
3 cooking apples

Put the oil in a sauté pan and place it over a medium heat. Salt the chicken pieces and fry them on all sides until golden. Take them out of the pan and set aside.

In the same oil, fry the onions, red pepper, garlic and carrots, first over a high heat, then reduce the heat to soften the vegetables. Add a little bit of salt. When the vegetables are soft, return the chicken to the pan. Wait for three minutes, then add the vinegar. Let it bubble for a couple of minutes, then add a glass of water (about 150ml) and the bay leaf. Cover the pan and let it all simmer for 30 minutes.

Core the apples and cut them into quarters. Add them to the pan, cover once again and let it all simmer for another 20 minutes until the apples are soft.

Chicken with garlic

You can find this recipe in most down-to-earth Spanish restaurants. Amazingly, it does not really taste a lot of garlic, even though it has a considerable amount in it. In any case, you should know that Spaniards are truly sensitive when it comes to garlic: the wife of a very famous footballer once said that the whole country smelled of garlic and, though that was many years ago, she has not been forgiven yet!

Serves 4

2 tbsp olive oil
sea salt
4 chicken thighs
6 garlic cloves, thinly sliced
3 tbsp sherry vinegar or red wine vinegar
2 bay leaves

Heat the olive oil and salt the chicken thighs. Fry them on all sides over a medium-high heat until they are a dark golden colour. Set aside.

Reduce the heat under the pan and wait for a while until the oil cools down. Then fry the garlic slices for a minute or so until they are a pale golden colour. Add the vinegar and let it bubble for another few seconds. Then add a glass of water (about 150ml) and the bay leaves. Let it all bubble for a minute, then return the chicken, reduce the heat and simmer for 20–25 minutes until the chicken is tender and cooked through.

Remove the bay leaves and serve with crusty bread (more authentically Spanish), or with rice (the way foreigners eat it, or, as the Spanish might say, *guiri*).

Roast chicken three ways

Just a few days after the coalition was formed, I was called to go to Number 10 for lunch so that 'the wives' would get to know each other. To the average sane person it would be plainly weird that, when your partner gets a new job, you would be asked for lunch with their colleague's partner... most people just get away with a dinner all together after a few months, if that. But this is the thing about politics: it is not really for average sane people!

The Prime Minister and his family had just been moved provisionally into the old Number 10 flat, while the new flat that is used now was being renovated and a kitchen was being installed, so they did not really have the equipment to prepare a meal. The lunch was a roast chicken on top of a wooden chopping board, an unwrapped packet of butter, a tube of Hellmann's mayonnaise and a box of Maldon salt.

This is how you roast chicken, whether you are in England, in Spain, at Number 10 or anywhere else.

With all these recipes, check the chicken is done before removing it from the oven. The easiest way is to insert a long sharp knife into the thickest part of the thigh. If the juices that emerge are tinged with pink, return it to the oven for five minutes before testing again. If the juices run clear, it is ready.

All recipes make 1 roast chicken

CHICKEN 1

1 chicken
sea salt
250g butternut squash, or sweet potatoes, or both, in chunks
2 onions, in chunks
3 tbsp olive oil

Cut off the leg joints at the knees and the wing tips (you can use them for chicken soup). Salt the chicken inside and out. Take a roasting tin, put the vegetables in with more salt and 2 tbsp of the oil, tossing them with your hands so that they are all coated. Then put the chicken in the tin, rubbing it with the remaining 1 tbsp of oil. Leave for 30 minutes. Preheat the oven to 200°C/400°F/gas mark 6.

Pour in a glass of water (about 150ml), taking care not to pour it over the chicken, and roast for 1¾ hours.

Continued overleaf...

CHICKEN 2

1 chicken
sea salt
1 lemon, halved, plus the juice of ½ lemon
4 potatoes, cut in 8 wedges lengthways
3 tbsp olive oil
1 tsp thyme or rosemary

Preheat the oven to 200°C/400°F/gas mark 6. Cut off the leg joints at the knees and the wing tips. Salt the chicken inside and out. Put the halved lemon in the cavity.

Take a roasting tin and add the potatoes, 2 tbsp of the oil, more salt, the juice of the ½ lemon and the herbs. Toss together and put the chicken on top, rubbed with the remaining 1 tbsp of oil.

Put it in the oven and, after 30 minutes, add a glass of water (about 150ml), taking care not to pour it over the chicken. Roast for 1¾ hours in total.

CHICKEN 3
And, finally, this is a very Spanish way.

1 chicken
sea salt
2 tbsp olive oil
3 tbsp white wine vinegar
1 tsp finely chopped parsley leaves

Preheat the oven to 200°C/400°F/gas mark 6. Cut off the leg joints at the knees and the wing tips. Salt the chicken inside and out, rub it with the oil and put it in a roasting tin.

Pour in a glass of water (about 150ml), taking care not to pour it over the chicken. Cook for 1¼ hours, then mix another glass of water with the vinegar and parsley and pour it over the chicken. Let it roast for another 30–40 minutes. Serve.

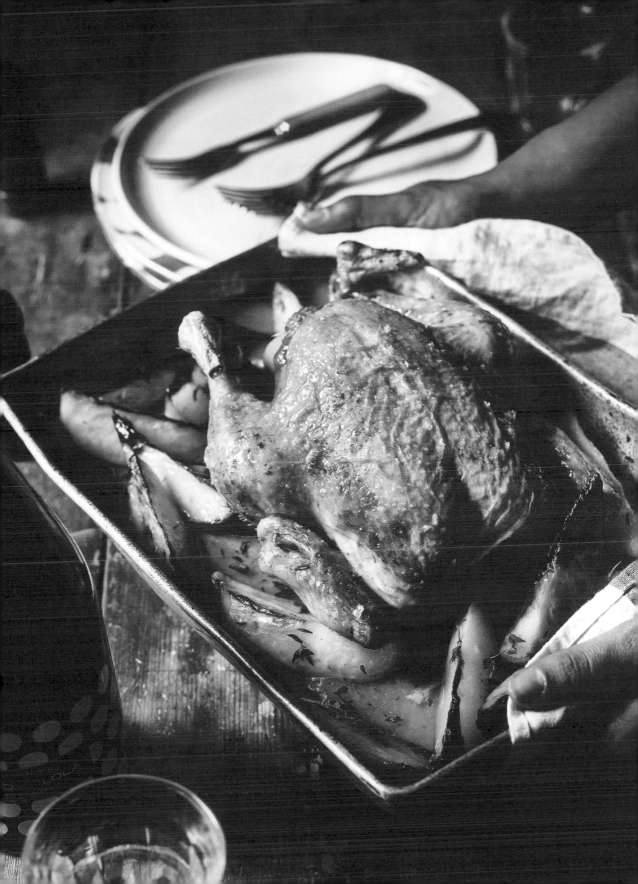

Partridges *estofadas*

Apart from being an amazing cook, my grandmother María cooked with love; you knew how much she loved you just by looking at what she had cooked for you, whether it was something you liked or not. I was her only goddaughter and, as a result, she often spoiled me. I spent a couple of weeks on my own with my grandparents every summer – long summers of hot lazy afternoons – and on the day when I arrived she normally prepared partridges *estofadas* hunted by my grandfather, my very favourite dish.

Hunting, for my grandfather, had nothing to do with the hunting expeditions that are organised by rich people nowadays; it was proper farmer's hunting. Truly the real thing. The partridges lived in the wheat fields that were almost ready for harvest. Those never-ending fields – with the yellow of the dry wheat, the red of the poppies and the intense blue of the open sky – are a painting in themselves. The painting of the Castilla land, the land where my heart is.

Serves 4

olive oil
sea salt
2 partridges
2 onions, finely chopped
1 carrot, finely chopped
½ red pepper, finely chopped

½ green pepper, finely chopped
4 garlic cloves, finely chopped
small handful of finely chopped
    parsley leaves
1 bay leaf
1½ tbsp sherry or red wine vinegar

Put enough oil in a frying pan to cover the base. Salt the partridges and fry them all over, sealing them until they are golden, then set aside. In the same pan add a little more oil and throw in the onions, carrot, peppers and garlic, parsley and bay leaf. Let it all fry over a medium heat until it is golden.

Return the partridges to the pan with the golden vegetables, add the vinegar and a glass (about 150ml) of water, cover the pan and let it simmer for 45 minutes. Take the lid off and there it is: the most delicious poultry you could possibly imagine.

My Christmas turkey

Christmas in Spain is actually celebrated on Christmas Eve. I have no idea how come so many Spanish families have started eating turkey, but I suspect it has to do more with the influence of Hollywood than anything else.

It took a while for Hollywood to make its way into my village but, when it did, it was mostly through Westerns. When I was little, the favourite actor was 'Juan Bayne' (John Wayne). And when I told my grandfather that I was going out with a Brit he kept asking me, 'How is the Indian?' as the only foreigners that he had seen in his whole life were the Native Americans in Spaghetti Westerns. Spain has really changed beyond recognition during my lifetime.

I like to very lightly marinate the turkey the day before cooking it by putting it in a (huge) bucket covered with a flavoured brine. For this, chop 2 onions and put them in the bucket with 1 chopped leek, 3 bay leaves, 2 halved mandarins, 1 halved orange, 1 halved lemon, a handful of parsley, 2 glasses of port (about 300ml), a handful of coarse salt and a handful of sugar. Add the turkey and cover with water. I am not sure this actually makes any difference to the final result, but my children, nephews and nieces like to help and it gets the magic of Christmas started.

Serves very many

1 turkey (the rule in my home is: the bigger the better)
sea salt
1.5kg apples (ideally of different kinds so you get different textures)
4 large onions
2 handfuls of pine nuts
150g prunes
150g dried apricots
100g raisins
100g unsalted butter, at room temperature
6 bay leaves
2 glasses of port (about 300ml)

Preheat the oven to 200°C/400°F/gas mark 6. If you have marinated the turkey, pat it dry. Salt it inside and out. Put the turkey in a (big) roasting pan. Peel and chop the apples in medium-sized chunks and the onions in slices. Mix the apples, onions, pine nuts, prunes, dried apricots and raisins and use some of this to stuff the cavity of the turkey, but don't put too much inside as air needs to circulate inside the bird.

Continued overleaf…

Now get the butter and work it between the skin and the breast, carefully opening up a cavity under the skin with your fingers and trying not to tear it. Massage the breast inside the skin with the butter. Arrange 3 bay leaves on each breast under the skin, then put the bird in the roasting tray breast side down. Arrange the remaining stuffing around the turkey. Dilute the port with water and throw it all over the turkey. You may need to add more water to the pan, the liquid should be more or less two fingers' depth.

Then start roasting, cooking for 45–50 minutes per kilo. Keep adding water if you think the roasting tin is getting dry. After 1¾ hours, put some foil over the sides of the turkey so that the stuffing on the tray does not get burnt. When there are 45 minutes left to go, turn the turkey over so it is breast side up. Test to see if it is done (see page 147); give it a few more minutes if it isn't quite there yet, then test again.

The turkey releases a lot of juice this way, so there is no need for gravy, but you may need to add a bit more salt to the sauce and stuffing before serving it. I serve it carved, with the stuffing and sauce separately on the side.

Russian steaks

I don't know why these are called Russian steaks as they do not seem to have anything Russian in them, but it is what we call them. It's an everyday dish for children in Spain.

In my grandparents' house we had this often for lunch. Usually after lunch you simply could not go out to the street, so hot was it, so the incentive to remain seated talking to the family (no electronic devices or TV being available at the time) was huge.

Now, let me tell you, I have participated in Middle East peace process discussions, negotiated with the Iranian government, led World Trade Organisation negotiations, handled seriously complex discussions on EU policy… but I have never, ever, had arguments as tough as those we had with my grandfather. He had strong opinions on everything and defended them with a stubbornness I have not witnessed since.

Our biggest arguments were about the theory of evolution, as he did not believe in it. I kid you not. I am even all worked up about it again now as I am writing about it.

We tried every possible argument to convince him, from complex biology and physics explanations that we had read in our school books to the simplistic, 'Because everybody says so!' Still, he did not concede an inch. His killer argument was: 'If men come from apes, why are there still apes?' Now, you try to answer that one!

Children love these and the coating helps to keep the meat moist so you can avoid side sauces such as ketchup. Serve them with pasta on the side, or just a green salad.

Serves 4

For the steaks
500g minced beef
4 tbsp breadcrumbs, plus more
    if needed
2 tbsp finely chopped parsley leaves
2 tbsp red wine vinegar
1 garlic clove, crushed
1 egg, lightly beaten
1 tsp sea salt
freshly ground black pepper

To coat and cook
olive oil (enough to coat the base of
    a frying pan generously)
plain flour, to coat
1 egg, beaten with 2 tbsp milk

Mix all the ingredients for the steaks well, with a spoon or with your hands. The quantities are a guide only and you can alter them as you wish. The mixture should not be wet though; if it is, just add more breadcrumbs. If you have time, chill the mixture for 20 minutes. This will help to shape the steaks, though if you do not have time it does not really matter.

Heat the oil in a frying pan until very hot. Put the flour and egg in two dishes.

With your hands, get bits of mixture of around the size of a golf ball. Coat them in flour. Flatten them, then coat them in egg, drain well, and fry them in batches. As soon as you put a batch in the pan, reduce the heat under it to medium. Also, remember not to pack too many steaks into the pan or the meat will boil rather than fry. Turn the steaks halfway through. They are ready when they are golden on both sides.

Roast lamb

In Castilla we pride ourselves on our roast lamb. We eat it plain: no garlic, no thyme, no rosemary… and definitely no gravy. But the price for that is that you can only cook this if you have a really good lamb.

I love this so much that it was the main course we served at our wedding. Mind you, the roast lamb of Segovia, where Nick and I celebrated our wedding, is simply epic.

Preheat the oven to 200°C/400°F/gas mark 6. Salt the lamb (we normally roast a whole lamb or half a lamb, but when we eat it we all fight for the shoulder, which is the very best cut) and put it on a roasting tray. Add a glass of water (about 150ml). Leave it in the oven for two hours and sprinkle the juice of ½ lemon on top of the lamb 20 minutes before it is done. That is all: we eat it immediately (none of this 'leaving it to rest' that people have invented nowadays). It is just divine.

Nick and me on our wedding day

Stewed lamb

If you only try one recipe from this book, let it be this. It is my eldest son's favourite dish. It was normally made by my grandma María with Churro lambs that my grandfather raised but, even if you make it with regular lamb, the taste is superb.

In Spain we eat lamb that is very young. I realise that for the average British reader this is likely to sound truly uncivilised – and it probably is – but the ideal lamb size in Spain is 5–7 kilos. A likely worse way to look at this is to say that lambs are killed when they are only 35 days old. Even my children, who have been lobbying unsuccessfully for a dog for the last four years, have views on this. When they asked me once whether they could at least get a micropig, my youngest asked, 'But promise you will not cook it!' That said, they have never been squeamish about eating the very delicious lambs when they are in Spain…

Serves 5

sea salt
5 lamb leg steaks
plain flour, to dust
olive oil
1½ garlic cloves
1 tbsp chopped parsley leaves
1 glass of white wine (about 150ml)
100–150g peas (frozen are fine here)
3 potatoes, cut into chunks

Salt the steaks and dust them with the flour. Fry them in a pan in a generous amount of olive oil until they are a little golden on both sides. Set aside. Discard half the oil that you used to fry the steaks.

Heat the remaining oil. Meanwhile, crush the garlic and parsley in a mortar and pestle, stirring in the glass of wine. Add it all to the oil and wait until there are bubbles on the surface (one minute or so). Pour in a glass (about 150ml) of water and wait until there are bubbles again. Now return the steaks and let it all simmer for 45–50 minutes, or until tender, over a low heat. Add the peas and simmer for another five minutes.

Separately fry the potatoes in olive oil until they are golden, then set them on kitchen paper to blot off any excess oil. Add them to the lamb and let them simmer all together for a final three or four minutes.

This dish, as is the case with all stews, tastes better a day after it is made.

Picadillo

My paternal grandma, Angela, was famous in her village for her chorizos. In the autumn my grandparents used to kill a pig so that the family would have charcuterie for the whole year: from chorizo to hams or salamis. This is called the *matanza* and it could involve the whole family, from little kids to grandparents, and often neighbours and friends as well, as it still does nowadays in many areas of Spain.

The *matanza* needed all hands on deck as there was a lot of work to be done: stuffing the chorizos, cutting the meat, marinating it, draining the blood, salting the hams... the children were often allowed to turn the mincing meat machine, but they were also around when the pig was killed, which really was not fun to see. No chance to avoid contact with the food chain in those days... When one hears of children these days who are asked to draw a picture of a chicken and they draw it roasted, it is obvious how much things have changed.

Serves 6–8

1kg pork shoulder and 50g pork belly, minced together
   (ask the butcher to mince them)
1½ tsp sea salt
1 garlic clove, very finely chopped
2 tsp sweet smoked paprika (*pimentón*)
2 tsp white wine
pinch of ground cumin
½ tsp good-quality dried oregano
1 tbsp olive oil

Mix all the ingredients except the oil in a bowl, cover and let them rest for 24 hours in the fridge.

Fry the mixture in a very large frying pan or a wok, in the olive oil, for anything from 10–20 minutes, stirring and turning until it starts getting a bit brown and is no longer pink.

Serve with fried eggs, or bread, or both, or just on its own.

Grilled steak

Teaching teenagers how to grill meat and fish is a must, as it means that they suddenly have more than six new dishes in their repertoire: beef, pork, lamb, haddock, cod, salmon…

Learning how to grill properly is actually more important – and difficult – than it seems: most people put far too much meat or fish in the griddle pan at once, and, as a result, steam accumulates and the cuts of fish or meat boil and become soggy rather than crisp-edged and delicious. Definitely not nice. Grill in small batches: much better.

Serves 1

1 thin beef steak
1 tbsp olive oil
½ lemon (optional)
sea salt

Heat a griddle pan until it is really hot. Coat the steak with the oil (do not add oil to the pan or it will produce tonnes of smoke).

Put the steak on the pan and grill for five minutes on one side and three on the other (this is really to taste, but as soon as children cook this three times they will learn quickly what timings work best for them).

If you wish you can drizzle a bit of lemon juice on top. Take the steak out of the pan, add the salt (if you add it before cooking, it will produce a lot of moisture that will have a boiling effect on the meat). Let it rest for five minutes, then eat.

Pig's cheeks in wine sauce

This is a truly gorgeous dish, and for very little money as well. Pig's cheeks are a very underrated cut: 500g feeds five people and costs less than £5 but, if you cook it properly, the meat is a real delicacy.

The most popular way to eat pig in Spain is to roast a whole piglet. The best place to eat this is in Segovia or in Arévalo, in Castilla, and it is so tender that the piglet is cut with a dish. (The dish is broken by throwing it against the floor, there never being a lack of theatrics in Spain!)

Many people also like to eat a whole roasted head of pig. If you do want to try this, preheat the oven to 200°C/400°F/gas mark 6, put the pig's head in the sink and clean it well, pour boiling water over the head at least three times to get rid of any germs, dry it well, add salt all around, cover the ears with foil and then put it into the oven for 1½ hours (ears side down). After that time turn the head around, uncover the ears and roast for another 1–1¼ hours.

If the head or the whole piglet is not for you, then try this much more civilised recipe which is divine. Ask the butcher to trim out the fleshy cushion parts of the cheeks, don't go home with whole cheeks (which are enormous).

Serves 4–5

sea salt
10 pig's cheeks
3–4 tbsp plain flour
4 tbsp olive oil
2 carrots, finely chopped
2 onions, finely chopped
1 garlic clove, finely sliced
1 celery stick, finely sliced
1 red pepper, finely chopped

1 leek, finely sliced
500ml red wine, or ideally 250ml red wine
    and 250ml sweet wine, such as Malaga,
    Pedro Ximénez, Marsala, or even port
small handful of parsley leaves,
    finely chopped
1 bay leaf
1½ tbsp red or white wine vinegar

Salt the cheeks, dust them with flour and fry them in the olive oil on both sides until they turn golden (a couple of minutes on each side). Take them out of the pan and set aside. Then add all the vegetables and fry them for five minutes over a medium heat. Return the cheeks, pour in the wine and a glass of water (about 150ml), add the parsley and bay leaf, wait until there are bubbles in the sauce, then cover with a lid, reduce the heat and let it simmer for one hour. Then add the vinegar and let it simmer for another 45 minutes. The result should be really tender, buttery meat in a thick sauce.

This tastes better if you eat it the following day. I serve it with potato cubes fried in olive oil (just heat the oil, fry the potato cubes for three minutes on each side, blot them on kitchen paper to get rid of the excess oil, then sprinkle with salt).

Gorgeous.

San Jacobos

You can make San Jacobos with pork or beef. They are a thin steak stuffed with Spanish ham and a slice of cheese. If you roll them instead, they become *flamenquines*, which are typical of the South of Spain.

I prefer to use pork leg steaks and, in order to make them as thin as possible, I hit them and roll them with a rolling pin, which is a fantastic way to get rid of stress.

Children love these.

Serves 4

sea salt
4 thin pork or beef steaks
4 slices of Serrano or Parma ham
4 slices of cheese (Gouda or Cheddar)
1 egg, lightly beaten
1 glass of very fine breadcrumbs
olive oil

Salt the steaks, then pummel them and roll them with a rolling pin to make them thin. Put a slice each of ham and cheese on top of each steak and fold them over. Put the beaten egg in a dish and the breadcrumbs in another. Coat the stuffed steak with the egg, then with the breadcrumbs. If you're making this for the first time and are nervous it might fall apart, you could always repeat these coatings, though remember that a thicker coating will be tougher.

Meanwhile, heat a generous amount of olive oil in a deep pan. Fry the steaks over a medium heat for four to five minutes on each side. Do not be tempted to cook these over a high heat as that will mean that the crumbs will turn dark golden before the layers of meat are properly cooked through.

Loin of pork

This is a really versatile and easy dish. People get over-complicated with roasting times. My mother's unscientific but foolproof formula is, 'Two hours for a big loin and two hours for a small one'. If you think that is bad, this is her timing for a chicken: 'Half an hour more than you think'!

This is a way to roast loin that makes a very pretty dish and which evokes the Moorish influence in Spanish cuisine. People often forget that Spain was under the rule of the Moors for 800 years (276 years more than under Christendom).

Serves 5

1 x 500g pork loin, skinned
handful of dried apricots, plus more if you like
handful of prunes, pitted, plus more if you like
sea salt
2 tsp dried oregano
2 onions, cut into big chunks
olive oil

For this dish you ideally need a clay roasting tray. I don't know what is the scientific explanation for this, but clay roasting trays keep the moistness in meat.

Preheat the oven to 250°C/475°F/gas mark 9. Make a hole shaped like a cross through the middle of the pork loin with a long knife; you may need to pierce it from both sides, but it is very easy to connect both holes. Stuff as many apricots and prunes as you can into the hole (I normally stuff one side with apricots and the other with prunes, but you can mix both). Rub the loin with the salt and the oregano. Put it in a – not too big – ideally clay roasting tray with the onions, throwing in a few more apricots and prunes if you wish. Drizzle olive oil on top and put it all into the oven for 15 minutes.

Add a glass of water (about 150ml) to the tray, not on top of the pork, and reduce the oven temperature to 190°C/375°F/gas mark 5. Let it roast for 1½ hours more or less, adding more water to the tray if it dries out. Let the loin rest for 20 minutes before you cut it into even slices.

You do not need any gravy for this as there are normally enough juices left in the roasting tray. In any case, as you may have already guessed by this point in the chapter, I never use gravy, whether in Spain or in the UK…

Me with my mother, father, sister and brother, in Austria, eating apricots

My father and brother in Segovia with a tiny roast suckling pig and a local restaurateur – the pork is so tender you can cut it with a dish

On a beach in Asturias with Nick, our young son and my sister

My paternal grandparents with their Fiat 1500, which is very significant in Spanish history as it was the first car that most people could afford

Passing it on

When my brother, sister and I were little, my parents used to tell us that the only things we would inherit from them were our education and their books. It turns out that was not true, as they also gave us a deep sense of belonging and a close-knit family. And a love of food.

I am Catholic and therefore I do not believe in reincarnation, but I promise you that every time I make my grandma's Stewed lamb recipe (see page 156), she is somehow there, in the kitchen, with me. I do not know whether it is the smell that conjures her, or just the fact of going through the cooking steps that she herself methodically always went through – in the same order and in the same way – but something happens in the kitchen that brings her to me. Likewise, every single time I make mayonnaise in my kitchen in London, I hear my mother's voice telling me to steady my hand, even though she lives no less than 1,300 kilometres away.

Giving that same sense of emotional belonging to my children is precisely the reason why I cook with them. I don't even care whether they learn the recipes by heart or if they actually manage to make them on their own. The pleasure of cooking with them is in being with them; in teaching them not about recipes but about food; in getting them to see that food is not just fuel, but something you share.

I come from a family of strong women (one ancestor was a female Colonel who backed the French occupation in the early 19th century – the traitor! – while her husband was a Colonel fighting against the French… talk about healthy competition between husband and wife.)

For decades, food in my family has been in the hands of women; the family recipes have been handed over from mother to daughter, then to granddaughter and great-granddaughter. So this is the very first time that I am passing on the recipes to three boys instead.

It is probably because I am cooking with sons and not with daughters that I initially thought I had to give them an additional incentive and so came up with the idea of creating a blog so that I could 'lure' them with the internet. Truth be told, we are now writing the blog out of habit and a certain feeling of commitment more than anything else. What my sons enjoy is not putting recipes on the internet, but spending the time together cooking, learning about where the recipes come from and experimenting with the ingredients as we go. An understanding of food and a collection of recipes and the stories around them is a treasure chest – one of the best gifts anybody could receive – and that is as precious for boys as it is for girls.

Now that I have spent more than four years cooking with my sons, I am not sure that boys and girls approach cooking in the same way, which somehow challenges my feminist convictions. There is indeed an awful lot of bashing, blending and pulverising food in my kitchen and very little delicate baking, folding or piping (not to mention the monumental mess they can make). But I am certain that food is getting into my sons' blood as deeply as it is in mine, no matter if they would rather carelessly pile up ingredients while I arrange them neatly.

My middle son has taken to cooking with particular interest and, as a result, I have had the additional pleasure of seeing how a child blossoms when they discover something they are really good at. One day he came down early in the morning for breakfast and, rather than rushing to the computer, he asked: 'So what are we going to eat today?' At that moment I could picture my mother and my grandmother smiling in the background, while I thought: 'We are there!'

A street in Seville with the Spanish flag

A dish of clams

Starting a paella

At the opening event of the female role models campaign

Recipes for children

These are the dishes to prepare children to feed themselves:

Tomato sauce (*see page 78*)
Chorizo omelette (*see page 74*)
Easy pasta with bacon and peas (*see page 182*)
Grilled steak (*see page 160*)
Pasta bake (*see page 185*)
Roast tomatoes (*pictured right, see page 91*)

*These are recipes for when you are fed
up with cooking and need a quick win:*

Cuban rice (*see page 180*)
Sausage bake (*see page 193*)

These are some recipes that are fun to make together:

Chorizo pinwheels (*see page 207*)
Bean quesadillas (*see page 209*)
Sherbet (*see page 198*)
Spherifications (*see page 200*)
Tomato and cheese loaf (*see page 217*)

*And these recipes are for when you need
to be the best mum in the world:*

Pancakes (*see page 218*)
Churros with chocolate (*see page 220*)
French toast (*see page 219*)
Lemonade (and pink lemonade) (*see page 241*)

*… And if you are in urgent and real need to score brownie points, just
ignore your conscience for once and open a bag of chilli Doritos.*

COMFORT FOOD
AND ONE-POT MEALS

As does any other country, Spain has its own list of family comfort foods, those that remind us of our childhood or of meals with family and friends. You will struggle to find any Spaniard who does not enjoy a bowl of *macarrones con tomate* (pasta with tomato sauce and chorizo), an *arroz a la cubana* (Cuban rice), or a dish of paella. All of those dishes are in this chapter.

And, much like everywhere else, each family has their own list of favourite meals, which either go down well with children or which remind us of a particularly fun or important time.

A favourite family comfort dish should tick the following boxes:

- filling
- not too expensive
- and easy to make

As far as I am concerned, one-pot meals are the ultimate comfort food. Indeed, I have observed over the years that the less mess there is to clear up, the more 'comforted' I am. Call me simple, but it is an empirical fact!

Paella

I am including this recipe in the book with reluctance, as Spanish people have been fighting ever since Franco died against the stereotype that Spain is just about 'paella, flamenco and sun'. Not even the South of Spain is like that.

Besides, I never cook paella, mostly because it is one of my mother's signature dishes, so we normally have it when we are in Spain with her.

Anyhow, pretty much every time I see a British cook making a paella recipe I find myself asking: what the hell is that? So let me give you some basic tips about the recipe... and also about the stereotypes:

About the stereotypes:

It is pronounced 'pa-ey-a' not 'pie-ella'.

We do not eat paella every single day, so there is no obligation to eat it every single day if you happen to be in Spain.

Paella is typically from Valencia and the area of Levant; in most other Spanish regions they just do not cook paella, almost ever.

We do not have it for dinner. Never. If you see anybody in Spain eating paella in the evening you can be sure they are foreigners (*guiris*, as foreigners are sometimes called in Spain). Or, more likely, a foreigner having an early dinner at 5pm, just as we are finishing our lunch.

And for the recipe:

Never, ever add chorizo to paella, it is plain weird. Honestly, not good.

Do not add ready-cooked fish, mussels or prawns: the whole point of paella is that the rice absorbs the flavours of the fish and seafood as they cook.

We normally use one handful of rice per person and one more 'for the pan'. The rice should be round, not long. In some Spanish shops you can find Calasparra rice; this is the very best, the *pata negra* of rices.

Cover the paella with a clean tea towel for a couple of minutes before serving: that prevents the rice from getting sticky. The rice in paella should be fluffy and dry.

It is strictly forbidden to sprinkle the paella with parsley or any other herb... what is the point of that??

Continued overleaf...

Serves 6 (or 5 hungry people)

10–15 clams, well scrubbed and
    soaked in salted water (see page 22)
6 mussels
12 raw prawns
1 fish bone (flat fish is best)
olive oil
1 onion, finely chopped
½ green pepper, finely chopped
1 red pepper, finely chopped
½ tomato, preferably peeled,
    finely chopped
2 garlic cloves, unpeeled

100g Serrano ham, finely chopped
½ tsp finely chopped parsley leaves
1 bay leaf
1 squid (or 6–7 frozen squid rings),
    chopped
1 slice of chewy fish (tuna, conger
    or monkfish), chopped into cubes
handful of frozen peas
½ lemon
500g Calasparra or other paella rice
sea salt
pinch of saffron threads

Boil two glasses of water (about 300ml) in a saucepan, add the drained clams, throwing away any with cracked shells or that are open and do not shut when tapped sharply on the sink, cover the pan with a lid and let it all boil for just a minute. Take the pan off the heat, strain the cooking liquid through a sieve and reserve it. Discard any clams that have not opened. Repeat the process with the mussels.

Peel the prawns; boil the fish bone and prawn shells in another two glasses (about 300ml) of water for 10–15 minutes. Pass this stock through a sieve and reserve it.

Cover a wide, shallow pan or paella pan with about a 1cm depth of olive oil and place over a medium heat. Fry the onion, peppers, tomato and garlic (in that order) for five minutes. Then add the ham, parsley and bay leaf, reduce the heat and keep cooking for another five to seven minutes until the whole thing becomes soft, slightly translucent and gooey. Increase the heat to medium once more, add the squid and then the fish and keep cooking it all for another five minutes. Finally add the prawns, the peas and half lemon (in one piece, not chopped). Keep frying it until the prawns take on a coral colour and the lemon turns brownish.

Now add the rice and the salt and move it all around a little bit with a spoon. After a couple of minutes (when the rice starts getting translucent) add the mussel and clam cooking liquid and the fish stock. Dissolve the saffron in half a glass (about 75ml) of boiling water and add it, too, to the pan. You should end up with 1cm of liquid on top of the rice, so add more water if needed until you have that. Let it all bubble and cook for 18–20 minutes. (If you wish you can do this last step in the oven, preheated to 200°C/400°F/gas mark 6.) As soon as you add the water to the rice you should not stir it any more or you will end up with a sticky mess rather than fluffy rice.

Five to eight minutes before you take it off the heat, add the clams and mussels.

Take the dish off the heat, cover with a clean tea towel and let it rest for two or three minutes. The rice should be a bit al dente.

Serve immediately. And when I say immediately I mean immediately. Most arguments in Spanish families happen when you have prepared a paella, the rice is ready and then somebody in the family arrives late. Unforgivable.

Pasta with chorizo *Macarrones con tomate*

A Spanish classic that comes from an Italian classic. In fact, when Spanish people say they will cook pasta, this is what they normally mean. My grandma went as far as boiling the pasta in the tomato sauce itself. I thought my Italian friends would be horrified to hear this, but I have found out that, in the old times, this is how pasta was prepared in some parts of Italy. Children love this dish, no matter what their age.

For as many as you like

dried pasta (preferably penne), 1½ handfuls per person
sea salt
Tomato sauce (see page 78), about ½ glass (75ml) per person
chorizo, cut into cubes, around 30g per person
grated cheese (any would do: Parmesan, Cheddar, or, if you want
    to be truly authentic, Manchego)

Boil the pasta in salted water following the packet instructions, then drain it. Mix it with the tomato sauce.

Meanwhile, fry the chorizo in a dry pan for two or three minutes (or microwave on a high setting for 45 seconds; we have a 700W oven). Discard the (considerable amount of) fat that oozes out. Mix the chorizo with the pasta. Sprinkle the cheese on top.

Fideua with squid

This a dish that comes from Valencia; it is essentially a paella made with pasta. It cooks in very little time and is both tasty and nutritious. My children like it with squid as it means they do not need to peel any prawns. Less prawns to peel, less mess: yes!!

You can prepare a fish stock very easily, by boiling a fish bone (a flat fish bone is best), a bay leaf and half an onion in water for 30 minutes, then straining the liquid.

Serves 5

3 tbsp olive oil, plus about 150ml for the pasta
1 onion, finely chopped
1 garlic clove, finely chopped
½ green pepper, finely chopped
½ red pepper, finely chopped
3 tbsp Tomato sauce (see page 78)
1 tsp sweet smoked paprika (*pimentón*)
1 squid, cut into 1.5cm squares
200g angel hair pasta, or vermicelli
150ml fish stock
sea salt

Heat the 3 tbsp of olive oil in a very wide, shallow pan or (ideally) a paella pan. Add the onion, garlic and peppers and let them fry over a low heat for seven to nine minutes until they are soft. Increase the heat to medium, add the tomato sauce and paprika, toss it all well and let it reduce for seven to eight minutes. Then add the squid, toss it all again and let the squid become firm (three minutes at most).

Preheat the grill. Then heat the 150ml of olive oil in a deep saucepan over a medium heat. Add the pasta, in batches of about one-third at a time, and toss it until it gets golden (a couple of minutes). Take the pasta out of the pan with a slotted spoon and put it on kitchen paper to blot off the excess oil. Repeat to gild all the pasta. Add the pasta to the squid pan and stir it in. Pour in the stock (it should not cover the pasta), taste for seasoning, adding salt if you like, then grill for three minutes.

Cuban rice *Arroz a la cubana*

A staple dish on children's menus in Spain. It is basically white rice with tomato sauce and a fried egg, but I think it is called 'Cuban' rice because in Cuba they eat this with fried plantain as well. The dish has proven it has a lot of merit, as it cannot have been easy to keep the 'Cuban' title all the way through the Spanish dictatorship. You may think that is weird (and you would be right: it is indeed), but even the name of the colour 'red' was forbidden, because of its political connotations. My grandma on my father's side used to make fried eggs, then add a tiny bit of red paprika to the warm frying oil and a spoon of vinegar and pour this red sauce over the eggs. These were called *huevos colorados* ('coloured' eggs) rather than 'red' eggs…

You can make this with good-quality shop-bought tomato passata, but you will be pushing it a bit… home-made tomato sauce is really best here.

Serves 1

50g white rice
1 tbsp olive oil
sea salt
Tomato sauce (see page 78)
1 egg

Just boil the rice (normally 20 minutes). I know you are thinking this is straightforward, which it is, but the key to making rice is to fry it in the oil for three-ish minutes first, then add 100ml of water for each 50g of rice all in one go and finally the salt. When you pour the water in you should hear a sudden bubbly hissing noise.

When the rice is done, cover it with a tea towel. When you are going to serve it (Spanish mums normally use a little cup to mould the rice into a 'mini mountain' on the plate), put the tomato sauce on the side. Fry an egg (see page 64). And enjoy.

Thai chickpeas

Thai food is just unheard of in my village, but I have come to love it and make it often for lazy Saturday dinners in London.

When the person responsible for economic policy in the government came to my home for a meal, I refused to cook for him. Not because I disagree with him (though I do – and thoroughly so – but I also admit he is the most interesting and intelligent person in that party, and probably the hardest working, too), but because a few days before the 2010 general election I was told by somebody I trust that he had gone to various editors' offices asking them to write negative personal stories about us. I may never know whether this was true, but I will never cook for a person who has tried to damage me or my family personally. So when he came to my house to discuss some issues of the day and eat a meal with my husband, I found an excuse to take my children out for dinner. My husband ordered him a Thai takeaway.

This is my home-made version of Thai food.

Serves 4

2 tbsp olive oil
1 tbsp grated root ginger
1 red chilli, very finely chopped
1 garlic clove, crushed or very finely chopped (you can put the ginger, chilli and garlic in a small food processor and mince them)
3 spring onions, finely sliced

400g can of coconut milk
200g butternut squash, in bite-sized chunks
150g sweet potatoes, in bite-sized chunks
400g jar or can of chickpeas, drained and rinsed
sea salt
2 tbsp chopped coriander (leaves and stems chopped separately)

Heat the oil. Fry the ginger, chilli and garlic for a couple of minutes over a medium heat. Add the spring onions. After a couple of minutes, when they are golden, add the coconut milk. As soon as the milk starts bubbling, add the squash and sweet potatoes. Reduce the heat and simmer for 15 minutes.

Stir in the chickpeas, salt and chopped coriander stems, wait for five minutes, then serve with the coriander leaves sprinkled on top.

Easy pasta with bacon and peas

This is one of the simplest pasta dishes you can make. For my children, it is the recipe they can cook even when I am not there. I taught them this dish when, during the 2010 election, I fell down and broke my elbow (a truly spectacular fall in the middle of a crowded street and in front of a whole terrace… but all I was thinking of was how lucky I was that there was no photographer in sight). As I came back home after waiting for hours at A&E for an X-ray, my middle son looked at my elbow, then at me, and asked, 'So who is going to cook, then?' Now that he has seen how his innocent question has led me to get them to cook for four years, to run a blog and to write a cookery book, he knows he had better be careful in the future about asking any other such questions!

As I do not always have crème fraîche in the fridge, I sometimes make this instead with single cream (150ml) or milk (also 150ml). We have also tried it with Philadelphia cheese (3 tbsp) and that was good, too.

Serves 4

enough pasta for 4 (we use spaghetti, but you can use any dried pasta)
sea salt
100g bacon lardons
1 tbsp olive oil
1 garlic clove, crushed (optional)
150g frozen peas
3 tbsp crème fraîche
grated Parmesan cheese, to serve

Boil the pasta in plenty of salted water, following the packet instructions, then drain it well.

Meanwhile, fry the bacon in the olive oil over a medium heat. After three minutes, when the bacon is a little golden, add garlic if you are using it (if you do not like garlic just disregard this step). Let it fry for just one minute, then add the peas and salt to taste. Wait for three or four minutes, then add the crème fraîche. Wait until you see bubbles appear. That is all there is to it.

Drain the pasta, mix it with the sauce and sprinkle some grated Parmesan on top.

I do not say this only because my children make it, but it is very, very delicious.

Pasta bake

This works really well if you have to feed a crowd of teenagers. My eldest is at that age when they can eat steaks in pairs… but, somehow, feeding this to him and his friends before they go to a football (Arsenal) match always seems to do the job. We live in hope that one day Arsenal will win the Premier League.

Tossing the veggies with the oil and then with the tomato sauce, and dipping the basil leaves in oil, is what children like most when making this recipe.

Serves 6–8 (or fewer teenagers)

3 red or yellow peppers
1 aubergine
2 courgettes
2 onions
sea salt
4 tbsp olive oil, plus more for the basil leaves
1kg dried pasta (penne or similar)
1 mug of Tomato sauce (see page 78); or good-quality tomato passata or just
  a 400g can of chopped tomatoes
3 handfuls of grated cheese (this is actually better with Cheddar rather
  than more expensive Parmesan)
6–8 basil leaves (just for decoration really)

Preheat the oven to 200°C/400°F/gas mark 6.

Cut all the vegetables into chunks and put them on a baking tray. Add salt and the 4 tbsp of olive oil and mix well, so each chunk is coated with salt and oil. Bake for 45 minutes, until the edges get brown.

Meanwhile, boil the pasta in salted water according to the packet instructions. Drain the pasta.

When the veggies are ready, toss them with the pasta and the tomato sauce, while you preheat the grill.

Put the pasta in a heatproof baking dish and sprinkle with the cheese. Dip the basil leaves in oil and put them on top. Grill for three or four minutes until the cheese is golden and molten.

Meatballs

I once got into trouble for saying publicly that men who treat women as equal have more courage. In fairness I said it less politely than that, as I did not even use the term 'balls' (to my mother's dismay). Luckily there are now many men who subscribe to my view and my hope is that they keep finding the courage to speak up.

After quite a bit of drifting and meandering trying to get used to public exposure, I decided in 2013 that having such exposure only made sense if I did something positive with it.

This is how my campaign for female role models was born. Which in turn is the reason for this book, as I am trying to launch a new international initiative, Inspiring Girls, and hoping to raise resources to fund my involvement in it.

I had the idea of getting together women and girls one August afternoon while I was in Spain. The way in which women are pigeon-holed and the labels that are so often attached to them (and to myself) had bothered me for a long time… but when I read that girls thought there are not enough role models for them, I thought it was time to stop sitting on the fence.

That very afternoon I took my laptop and sent an email to 10 outstanding women (most of whom I knew, but others whom I had never met) and asked them whether they would agree to launch with me a female role models campaign. As I started drafting and sending the emails I realised this was going to be a success: by the time I had sent all 10 emails, eight of the women had already said yes.

Having recruited around 24,000 women volunteers all around the country, staged events with women in most sectors, won the support of some of the biggest companies and media groups, and involved more than 300,000 state school girls, it is now time to undertake a new challenge and launch a truly international campaign, so that we can connect female role models and girls no matter where they both are.

In fairness, it has been a lot of work, but meeting all those women, learning their stories, witnessing their generosity, seeing the effect they have on the girls (and the effect the girls have on the women!), being able to spend time with those wonderfully enthusiastic girls, who just need a tiny push, and being able to share a bit of their dreams… all that, all that is not just worth five years of public exposure, all that is probably worth my entire life.

Every nation has its version of meatballs; this is how we make them at our house.

Makes enough for 4

500g minced beef
1 egg, lightly beaten, plus 1 egg
  beaten with 1 tbsp milk, to coat
1 tbsp white wine vinegar
2 handfuls of breadcrumbs
sea salt
2 garlic cloves

3½ tbsp chopped parsley leaves
around 100g plain flour
olive oil
1 onion, finely chopped
1 glass of white wine (about 150ml)
1 bay leaf

Mix the meat, the 1 egg, the vinegar, breadcrumbs and two pinches of salt. Crush one of the garlic cloves and 1½ tbsp of the parsley in a mortar and pestle and add them to the mixture. Mix well with your hands. Take handfuls of the mixture and shape them into balls (each the size of a golf ball, more or less).

Put the flour in one dish, and the beaten egg and milk in a second. Season both. Heat enough oil to coat the base of a frying pan over a medium-low heat.

Now, take a meatball, coat it in flour, then coat it in the egg. Drain well and fry in batches of six or seven (do not over-cook, you just need to get them a little bit brown on all sides). Remove from the pan and repeat until you have fried all the meatballs.

Separately heat more olive oil and fry the onion slowly until it becomes translucent (seven to eight minutes). Crush the remaining garlic clove in a mortar and pestle with the remaining 2 tbsp of parsley. Stir the white wine into the garlic mixture and pour it all into the onion pan, increasing the heat to high and seasoning to taste. Add a glass of water (about 150ml) and the bay leaf. Heat until you see bubbles, then add the meatballs to the pan, reduce the heat to very low and simmer for 10–15 minutes.

Remove the bay leaf and eat with plain rice or crusty bread. My grandma used to add little cubes of fried potatoes to the simmering pan for three or four minutes, so that they would get soft and 'catch the flavour' of the meatballs.

Working with the Inspiring Women Campaign and the RAF in Manchester

Coca

The Spanish equivalent to pizza, but made with lard, which gives it a more crumbly consistency and a crisp, pastry-like crust. As with pizza itself, this recipe kind of brings the domestic side of you to the surface in a rather effective way, as the kneading is minimal and yet it gives you the illusion of baking bread. As for the children, if yours are like mine, they get a much bigger thrill when you simplify your life and order a couple of pizzas over the phone or online…

Makes 1 / Serves 6

For the dough
300g plain flour
50ml olive oil, plus more for the tray and for topping
80g lard, at room temperature, chopped
20g unsalted butter, at room temperature, chopped
7g fast-action dried yeast
pinch of sugar
pinch of sea salt

For the toppings
2 onions, finely chopped
3 tomatoes
handful of grated cheese

Preheat the oven to 200°C/400°F/gas mark 6.

Mix all the dough ingredients with 100ml of water and knead a little until you get a ball of dough. Let the dough rest for 20–30 minutes in a bowl covered with cling film. Oil a rectangular baking tray (usually about 30 × 20cm) and push out the dough on it with your fingers until the whole tray is covered.

Toss the onions in oil and put them on top (I often fry them lightly first as my children prefer them to be soft). Slice the tomatoes, coat them with olive oil and put them on top of the onions. Sprinkle with salt, then with cheese and bake for 30 minutes. Eat hot or warm.

Beans with clams

Now, this is a family secret: Asturias, in the North of Spain, is one of the most stunning places in Europe, but very few people know it. We went there on holiday as a family for pretty much every year of the coalition... and without a single incident with the media. There are no big buildings by the beach, no paparazzi, no fancy cafés, no menus with translations into three languages, no oligarchs with tacky yachts, no other politicians in sight... a truly authentic place. If you like sports as much as my family does, the fun is endless: in just one day you can trek up proper mountains with snow at their tops, jump in the crystalline waters of a mountain river, spend the afternoon on a wonderful beach, and have dinner in a little fishing village. The fact that Asturian food is some of the best in Spain helps, too.

Holidays for politicians often involve some sort of negotiation with photographers. You agree to a choreographed picture (often just having a coffee) and, in exchange, they leave you in peace for the rest of your holiday. Sometimes the photographers do not respect these terms and it is hard to describe the anger you feel when people take pictures of your children when you have not authorised them. Having said that, it is also true that some politicians have a tendency to go on holiday where every single paparazzi is: getting into swimming trunks in Marbella or Ibiza (beautiful as those places may be) is like getting into swimming trunks in the middle of Trafalgar Square.

This is a very typical Asturian dish. If you have good fish stock (see page 22), it will taste even better.

Serves 6

500g dried white beans
sea salt
½ green pepper
1 onion, halved
2 garlic cloves, unpeeled
2 tbsp olive oil
1 bay leaf
pinch of sweet smoked paprika (*pimentón*)
pinch of saffron threads
¼ tsp finely chopped parsley leaves
800g good clams, well scrubbed and soaked in salted water (see page 22)
½ glass of white wine (about 75ml)

Soak the beans in water overnight. Then drain them, put them in a big saucepan with enough water or stock to cover, the salt, green pepper, onion halves and whole garlic cloves, olive oil and bay leaf. Let it come to the boil, then reduce the heat to its lowest and let it simmer for at least two hours (it takes up to two and a half hours, the precise time depends on the quality of the beans, but they should be silky and soft as butter).

After one hour, throw in the paprika, saffron, parsley, more salt and also a glass of cold water (in Asturias this is said to 'scare the beans' and make them softer). Throw in another glass of cold water after another 30 minutes. Take the pepper, garlic cloves and onion out with a bit of the cooking liquid and blend them, then return this to the pan.

Separately (and after the beans are cooked) cook the clams. Discard any clams with cracked shells, or that are open and do not close when tapped sharply against the sink. Heat a frying pan, then add the drained clams and the wine. Cover and wait until the clams open up (discard those that do not), then put them on top of the beans and strain in their cooking liquid through a sieve, to remove any grit or sand. Serve immediately.

Leftover chicken pie

This is great with leftovers from a roast chicken, though you can of course cook the chicken from scratch if you prefer. Children always like this, and it is useful for them to learn that you are not meant to throw away leftover food. In Spain, the equivalent of this would be using up leftover chicken in *croquetas* (see page 43) but, while you will spend hours making *croquetas*, this is ready in no time.

Serves 4

2 tbsp olive oil
20g unsalted butter
2 leeks, chopped
1 garlic clove, finely chopped
100g bacon or ham, finely chopped
leftover roast chicken (whatever
  you have), cut into chunks

frozen peas (to taste, we added a couple
  of handfuls)
pinch of sea salt
2 tbsp crème fraîche or double cream
1 sheet of ready-rolled puff pastry
1 egg, lightly beaten

Preheat the oven to 200°C/400°F/gas mark 6.

In a shallow pan, heat the olive oil and butter. Add the leeks and garlic and let them cook over a low heat until the leeks become translucent. Add the bacon. Increase the heat to medium and add the chicken, then the peas and salt. Let it all cook for five minutes. Add the cream and let it bubble up for a couple of minutes.

Put the chicken and leek mixture into a pie dish. Cover it with the puff pastry. Prick it all over with a fork and brush it with the beaten egg so that it gets a nice golden colour. Put the dish into the oven and in 20 minutes it should be ready.

Sausage bake

Perfect for a lazy, cold afternoon. It is full of calories, and though I am normally into healthy food, even my will breaks down in front of this dish. Now, here's the bad news for those who are used to dieting like me: putting a little floret of broccoli on the side of this does not take the calories away… yes, I am sure of this… and yes, damn!

Serves 6

2 carrots, finely chopped
1 large onion, finely chopped
2 celery sticks, finely chopped
1 tbsp olive oil
sea salt
10 sausages
400g can of chopped tomatoes in natural juice
1 tbsp crème fraîche (optional)
4 slices of cheese (mild Cheddar, Edam, Gouda, or similar)

Preheat the oven to 220°C/425°F/gas mark 7.

Put the vegetables on a baking tray, mix them with the olive oil, add the salt and cook them in the oven for 15 minutes. Then add the sausages and return them to the oven for 25–35 minutes, or until they start getting golden on one side (this really depends how thick the sausages are). Turn the sausages, add the tomatoes mixed with the crème fraîche (if using) and return it to the oven for another 20–25 minutes, until the sauce gets a bit thicker.

Just before serving, put the cheese on top and put it all under a hot grill for a couple of minutes, until it turns dark golden.

Serve with pasta, or beans, or just on its own (given the amount of calories in this, probably best).

Pisto

On the day of the last general election, after a whole day trying to get people out to vote under the heavy rain in Sheffield, Nick and I went back home on our own. We were meant to have a light bite to eat before we went to the electoral count, which often happens in Sheffield really late into the night.

We switched on the television to see the exit polls. Though in politics you are ready for all that may come at you, they were such a shock that I couldn't even swallow a bite.

As we saw the first numbers we looked at each other and we did not even need words to know what had to be done. Nick started writing his resignation speech. We then tried to muster as much dignity as possible to go to the count and thank all the many people – who had spent months if not years working for the party – as warmly as they deserved. We used all our remaining will not to break down when people kept coming to hug us with desolate faces and in tears. We were taken back to London on a flight. I left Nick at a hotel where he finished his speech. While he delivered it, I rushed back to talk to the children, to explain what had happened and to ensure all was fine with them.

Life goes on, so when Nick came back later that evening, we sat around the kitchen table for a meal.

So that is how it ends…

…Or perhaps how it begins.

This is the pisto that my mother (who had come to help us during the general election) cooked for us that evening. As you can no doubt imagine, it is a truly comforting Spanish dish.

Serves 4

olive oil	2 large tomatoes, chopped
3 large onions, sliced	5 courgettes, cut into thick slices
1 red pepper, chopped	sea salt
½ green pepper, chopped	1 bay leaf
2 garlic cloves, finely sliced	4 eggs, fried (see page 64, optional)

Heat the olive oil in a frying pan over a medium heat. Fry the onions. As soon as they are a bit golden (12–15 minutes), add the peppers and garlic and let them fry for five to eight minutes. Then add the tomatoes and fry them for another three or four minutes. Reduce the heat to its minimum and let it all soften for 10 more minutes. Then put it in a serving dish and reserve.

Add a touch more olive oil to the pan and fry the courgettes for seven to eight minutes. As soon as they are ready, return the onion and tomato mixture to the pan. Add salt and the bay leaf and let it all bubble for 10–15 minutes over a low heat. If you get lots of liquid, increase the heat and let it evaporate for another 10 minutes or so. Do not stir too much, as you should keep the shapes of the vegetables.

You can eat this with fried eggs, grilled meat, grilled fish, or just with crusty bread. The children like it with grated cheese sprinkled on top, then melted under a hot grill.

A BIT OF FUN

Cooking is not just about producing nice food, or about sharing, it is also about having a little fun. Children tend to like experimenting with food and – provided they do not ruin expensive ingredients – there is nothing wrong with that.

From time to time I try with my kids some 'science-y' recipes – whether making sherbet, or spherifications with sodium alginate – and those often become the recipes they remember the most. And, of course, fruit gums will be the closest you can get to creating Haribo in your own kitchen, and to make them think that you are the best mother in the world… If you want to get children cooking, you could do worse than showing them these three recipes.

Sherbet

Not only something that every child likes, but also a good way to teach them about acids and alkalis. Naturally, you can change the colours and flavours of the sherbet by using orange, lemon or strawberry jelly powder.

Makes 1 glass (enough for 4 children)

2 tsp citric acid (you can buy this in your local chemist)
2 tsp bicarbonate of soda
½ sachet of raspberry jelly powder
4 tsp icing sugar

Mix all the ingredients well; if you get lumps pass it all through a sieve. When the sherbet mixes with saliva (a neutral substance), it produces a tickling effect. You can also put a spoonful of the sherbet into a glass of water so the kids can see how it becomes a fizzy drink.

Fruit gums

If you are in the new wave of parenting you may use 'incentives' with your kids, which in the old days were simply called 'bribes'. Still, sometimes only a sweet will do. If you find yourself with free time one day, these are fun to make. They have tonnes of sugar, though.

Makes about an ice cube tray full

23g flavoured jelly powder (we used raspberry)
25g gelatine powder
150ml fruit juice (we used apple juice)
75g caster sugar, plus more to dust
sunflower oil, or other flavourless vegetable oil, for the moulds

Put all the ingredients except the oil in a small saucepan, mix them well and heat for five minutes, stirring from time to time, until everything dissolves. Do not let it boil.

Meanwhile, oil silicone moulds well with sunflower oil (we used ice cube trays to make cubes). You really need to oil them well or the gums will not come out smooth.

Pour the jelly mixture over the oiled moulds, wait for three or four hours (no need to put this in the fridge), then unmould. You can roll the gums in caster sugar, but they are very nice on their own, too.

Spherifications

If your kids are into experimenting with food, you just have to try a few of the wonderfully innovative Ferran Adrià techniques. Adrià is the guy responsible for igniting the molecular gastronomy movement at his world-famous restaurant (sadly now closed), El Bulli, in Catalonia. Though we would never dream of making this for lunch, it is a fantastic thing for children to see. Being curious about innovation and change is as important in the kitchen as it is in life itself.

The yogurt variety are probably the easiest spherifications to make, as they do not require any additional calcium. You can also make spheres with fruit or vegetable purées (though you need to add calcium to the purée first).

Makes more than enough for an experiment and a snack!

7g sodium alginate (buy this online)
100g full-fat yogurt
icing sugar (optional, to sweeten the yogurt; if you use flavoured
    yogurt you will not need any)

Mix one litre of water with the alginate in a blender, whisking it well, and wait for at least 20 minutes (even better, overnight).

Mix the yogurt and icing sugar, if using. Drop small spoonfuls of yogurt into the alginate mixture. You may need to discard the first few as they come out in weird kidney-like shapes, but once you have done two or three it is easy to get the hang of it. Wait for a couple of minutes and you will see that a thick membrane has formed on the outside of the yogurt.

Remove the yogurt balls carefully from the alginate solution and 'clean them' by dropping them in a bowl of clean cold water. Remove them from the water and put them on kitchen paper to blot off the excess moisture. That is all.

We are not really into molecular cuisine, but these are interesting as they 'explode' in your mouth and the whole thing seems like edible chemistry to the kids.

SNACKS

Spanish people tend to have a somewhat loose relationship with daily routine, especially as regards meal times. Sitting at a bar terrace during a hot summer at midnight while the children run around? No worries, just ensure you are doing it while you eat an ice cream. Come home after a night out at 7am? That's fine, just stop at a *churrería* on the way and buy dough sticks to dip into cups of thick hot chocolate. Finish lunch at 5pm? Totally normal (in fact what we do not find normal at that time is to eat finger sandwiches and drink tea). But drink alcohol on an empty stomach? That, never! Little bits of food here and there are therefore needed each day to cope with the vagaries of slightly crazy Spanish time-keeping.

Snacks are increasingly becoming part of the everyday routine of most family households around the world.

These are some of the dips, treats and stomach fillers that we like.

Migas

Going out in Spain is something else. We always call the last drink 'the penultimate', in the hope that somebody will suggest that the party should go on.

I believe in hard work, but also in having fun. Proper fun. Once I dress up and go out you will struggle to get me back, especially if there is dancing in prospect.

Migas are there precisely for those moments when you come home seriously late with friends, desperate for food before you call it a day. They are the most wonderful combination of carbohydrates and fat (and, if you have been dancing, all those calories are OK for once). My children are very grateful that I have passed this recipe on to them for whenever they go clubbing in the future. Wisdom food is what this is...

Originally, *migas* were shepherd's food from Castilla, the main plateau in Spain, though posh Spanish restaurants serve them as a starter now. The best bread to use is the white bit of baguettes, broken down with your fingers, but a good-quality regular loaf of bread is fine, too.

Serves 4 as a snack (or 20 if you guys are on a diet)

¼ tsp sea salt
4 handfuls of torn-up bread
3 tbsp olive oil
2 garlic cloves
½ red pepper (or even better a dried Spanish pepper called '*ñora*')
60g bacon or pancetta lardons
60g chorizo, chopped
pinch of sweet smoked paprika (*pimentón*)
handful of green grapes, halved

Dissolve the salt in a quarter glass of water (about 40ml) and sprinkle it (not too much) over the cubed bread. Put it on kitchen paper and press firmly so you get rid of the excess moisture. Heat the oil in a big frying pan. Fry the garlic cloves and pepper for five minutes over a low heat. Discard the garlic and pepper.

In the same oil, fry the bacon and chorizo for another three or four minutes, then add the paprika and finally the bread. Fry it all over medium heat for eight-ish minutes, until the bread is golden. Take it off the heat and add the grapes (I know it is a bit weird to add grapes, but it really works well).

Chorizo pinwheels

This is a very quick snack for the children, that does not really qualify as a recipe, but which they all love, especially if you serve it warm.

Serves 4 children as a snack

1 sheet of ready-rolled puff pastry
a little plain flour
150g chorizo, cut into small cubes
3 handfuls of grated cheese
1 egg yolk (optional)

Unroll the puff pastry sheet over a lightly floured surface. Sprinkle half the chorizo and half the cheese on top. Fold the pastry once and pass a rolling pin over it so that the cheese and chorizo stick to the pastry. Sprinkle the rest of the chorizo and cheese over the pastry, fold it again and press again with the rolling pin. Then roll the pastry so that you end up with a cylinder. Put in into the fridge for 15 minutes.

Preheat the oven to 200°C/400°F/gas mark 6.

Cut the pastry roll into slices (1cm thick, more or less) and put them on a baking tray lined with baking parchment, pressing them down gently. Brush them with egg yolk if you wish, but it is not really necessary. Bake for 20 minutes until golden.

Guacamole

Mexican food is increasingly popular in Spain, as indeed it is worldwide. I was first introduced to guacamole when I helped to negotiate the EU-Mexican trade agreement and I fell in love with it (as well as with margaritas, it is fair to say…).

Despite the fact that I have been cooking with my children for more than three years now and have introduced them to more than 200 recipes and all sorts of food, during a school parents' evening I had the humiliation of reading how my youngest son had said (in writing!) that his favourite food was… chilli Doritos. On the principle that if you can't beat them, join them, I decided to show them how to make guacamole to go with them.

Serves 6 as a dip

2 ripe avocados
juice of 1½ limes
sea salt
½ chilli, deseeded and very finely chopped
1 tomato, deseeded and very finely chopped
1 spring onion, very finely chopped
2 tbsp sour cream, or 1½ tbsp cream cheese
handful of coriander leaves, chopped

Peel and pit the avocados. Mash them with a fork and add the lime juice immediately so that they do not lose their green colour. Add all the other ingredients and mix well.

Open a bag of Doritos (chilli Doritos really are best).

Bean quesadillas

My eldest son has had an obsession with Mexico ever since, in Year 3, he did a project at school on a Mexican village called Tocuaro. It is a village of 600 people, so after a couple of weeks working on the project it felt as if we all knew by heart the name of every single inhabitant.

I am hoping he gets the same level of knowledge about Berlin next…

Makes 2

100g dried black or red beans
pinch of bicarbonate of soda
   (optional)
1 bay leaf
sea salt
1 onion, halved
2 tbsp olive oil
1 garlic clove

½ tsp ground cumin
½ tsp cayenne pepper
½ tsp dried oregano
4 Mexican tortillas (they
   sell them in all supermarkets)
2 handfuls of grated cheese
1 tsp chopped coriander

The night before you are going to cook the quesadillas, put the beans in a bowl and cover them with water (if you bought the beans some time ago, add a pinch of bicarb). Leave the beans in the water overnight. The following day, drain off the soaking water and put the beans in a pan, then cover with fresh water. Add the bay leaf, salt and half the onion and bring to the boil over a high heat. Boil for 10 minutes, then reduce the heat and let it simmer for 1½–1¾ hours. (We did this in the pressure cooker so it only took 30 minutes.) In any case, drain the beans and discard the onion and bay leaf. If you want to skip this step completely, just buy a can of red beans (in fact I only went through this process to show my son how to cook dried beans).

In a frying pan, heat the olive oil. Finely chop the remaining half onion and fry it for three or four minutes over a low heat so it becomes soft and translucent. Grate the garlic, add it to the pan and fry for three more minutes, then add the cumin, cayenne and oregano. After one more minute add the beans and 2 tbsp of water. Mash the beans a bit with the back of a fork or a potato masher. Increase the heat to maximum and, after two or three minutes (when the water has evaporated), the beans are done.

Heat a non-stick pan. Put a tortilla in the pan (no need to add any oil). Add half the bean mixture, then put a handful of grated cheese on top of the beans and sprinkle with half the coriander. Put another tortilla on top. Wait for two or three minutes until the bottom tortilla is golden, then flip it over with the help of a spatula. Let it get golden on the other side (a couple of minutes) then serve it, cut into quarters, while you repeat the cooking to make another quesadilla.

I like these on their own but you can serve them with Guacamole (see left), or salsa.

Aubergines with *salmorejo*

If you have some leftover *Salmorejo* (see page 39), you can easily make this dish, which is a really good way to get children to eat aubergines, a vegetable with which, for some reason, they often struggle. I love aubergines and I love *salmorejo*, so I 'double love' this dish.

Serves 2–3 as a snack

sea salt
1 aubergine, cut in rounds 5mm thick
chickpea (gram) flour (if you do not have this then use plain flour, but the
    aubergines won't be as crispy)
1 egg, lightly beaten
generous amount of olive oil
Salmorejo (see page 39)

Salt the aubergine slices and coat them with flour in a dish. Pour the egg into a second dish and coat the floured aubergines with the egg. Drain well.

Heat the olive oil in a non-stick frying pan and fry the aubergines until they are golden, turning them so that they become golden on both sides (it should take two or three minutes on each side). Take them out and place them on kitchen paper to blot off the excess oil.

Serve them with *salmorejo*: dip the aubergines in the *salmorejo* as you eat. The acidity of the vinegar in the *salmorejo* works really well with the oily aubergines.

Ham and cheese roll

This seems more difficult than it is. An aunt of mine often makes it for all the kids of the family when we are in Spain. But if you leave it in the fridge you will discover that it disappears by the end of the day, so you can assume that adults like it as well.

Makes 1 roll

unsalted butter, for the tray (optional)
3 eggs
80g caster sugar
80g self-raising flour
small (180g) tub of cream cheese
150g sliced ham

Preheat the oven to 200°C/400°F/gas mark 6. Butter a 30 × 20cm Swiss roll tray and line it with baking parchment (or use a silicone tray that does not need to be buttered or lined).

Beat the eggs and sugar together well with electric beaters until the mixture becomes light, thick and foamy. Then fold in the flour, trying not to lose too much air. Pour the mixture into the prepared tray. Bake for nine minutes.

As soon as you take it out of the oven, turn it on to a damp tea towel and roll it. Let it cool down, still rolled inside the towel, for about 15 minutes.

When it has cooled down, unroll it, spread with cream cheese and put the ham slices on top. Roll it again, pressing it firmly to get rid of any air pockets inside.

Wrap the roll in cling film or foil and store it in the fridge until ready to eat.

Courgette fritters

Another good recipe for teenagers to learn, as it is cheap, filling and healthy (well, healthy-ish). You can also make this with carrots, potatoes… or any combination.

You can eat these on their own, or with pesto, houmous, or yogurt sauce (mix yogurt with sea salt, lemon juice and finely chopped mint leaves).

Makes about 8

3 courgettes, coarsely grated
1 potato, coarsely grated
2 eggs, lightly beaten
½ garlic clove, finely grated
50g self-raising flour
handful of chopped parsley leaves
pinch of freshly grated nutmeg
sea salt
olive oil

Mix all the ingredients except the oil in a large bowl. Heat enough olive oil in a frying pan to coat the base.

Drop spoonfuls of the mixture into the oil, but do not crowd the pan, about four will be enough. Wait for two or three minutes until the fritters become a golden colour underneath, then flip them, fry them on the other side (also until golden), then take them out. Put them on a plate lined with kitchen paper to blot off the excess oil, then serve them or keep them warm while you cook the rest.

One of the few photos I have of the political side of my father's life. This is when he stood for election after the UCD collapsed and the liberals became part of the PP party

Fried chickpeas

When President Suarez of Spain died, in 2014, I was asked to accompany Nick to the official funeral. Suarez was my hero when I was little and for a long while when I got older, too. I think I might have had a proper crush on him because, apart from being a great politician, he was very handsome as well.

I was, from a very early age, engaged in politics, as my father had joined the centre party UCD and was very active in the transition to democracy. In fact, two of my earliest political memories are being outside the political rallies handing out green and orange stickers, the colours of the UCD, and then being back at home with my father, listening to Radio Paris, a radio channel that we could only hear intermittently because of the appalling radio signal, but was nevertheless a more reliable source of information on what was happening in our country than any of the official radio channels in Spain.

Suarez was the kind of person who, in a really difficult situation for Spain, did what he had to do, not what was good personally for him. And he did it even though he had to pay a massive political price, as in the 1982 election his party went from 168 MPs to just 11. Nobody in politics has done anything as generous for my country ever since. His resignation speech was of such dignity that I remember I cried rivers when I first heard it on TV… still, if you mention that speech to me, you will see tears in my eyes.

He was a very frugal man who liked fried chickpeas (leftover food in Spain). In Spain this meant making a *cocido* (boiling vegetables, dried chickpeas and meat for hours, see page 32), then frying the chickpeas in olive oil. This is a slightly more modern recipe, using chickpeas from a can.

Serves 4 as a snack (though they're very moreish)

3 tbsp olive oil
½ onion, finely chopped
1 garlic clove, crushed
400g jar or can of chickpeas, drained and rinsed (or use boiled chickpeas
   if you have them)
1 tsp red wine vinegar
1 tsp sweet smoked paprika (*pimentón*)

Heat the olive oil in a frying pan and fry the onion. When it is soft, add the garlic and chickpeas. If you are using jarred or canned chickpeas, be very careful because they will splatter everywhere, so cover the pan with a lid until this stops. Fry for 15 minutes. They should become golden.

Take them off the heat, sprinkle the vinegar and paprika on top, toss well and serve.

Cheese biscuits

My children call these 'magic biscuits' because one minute they are on the table and the next minute they have all disappeared. I call them 'magic biscuits' too, but for a very different reason: because one minute they are in your mouth, and the next five years on your hips!

Makes about 16

50g unsalted butter, softened
150g grated Manchego or Cheddar cheese
a couple of tbsp grated Parmesan cheese
100g plain flour
½ tsp dried thyme

Mix the butter and both cheeses, then work in the flour and thyme. Roll the mixture into a sausage shape. Wrap in cling film and chill it for 30 minutes to one hour.

Preheat the oven to 200°C/400°F/gas mark 6.

When the dough is cold, cut it into 1cm slices and place the slices on a baking sheet, pressing them down slightly. They take 10–15 minutes to bake golden and ready.

They are addictive, both warm and cold.

Tomato and cheese loaf

The good thing about this savoury cake is that you can use it to teach children how to pair flavours. Just stick to the basic recipe and simply replace the cheese, sun-dried tomatoes and basil with any other combination the children think might work: ham and cheese; spinach and pine nuts; butternut squash, pine nuts and goat's cheese; salami, olives and oregano… it really is up to them. If you want to try the more Spanish version of this, add chorizo, black olives and feta cheese… superb.

Makes 1 loaf

100ml olive oil, plus more for the tin
3 eggs, lightly beaten
225g self-raising flour
100ml white wine
sea salt

3 handfuls of goat's cheese,
    cut into little cubes
3 handfuls of sun-dried or SunBlush
    tomatoes, cut into small chunks
5 basil leaves, chopped

Preheat the oven to 170°C/340°F/gas mark 3½. Oil a 900g capacity loaf tin.

Mix the eggs, flour, wine, oil and salt. Then add the cheese, tomatoes and basil and mix well but carefully, so that you do not break up the cheese. Put it into the prepared tin and cook for 50 minutes, or until a skewer inserted into the centre comes out clean.

Let it cool down in the tin for about 10 minutes before you turn it out. Leave until just warm before cutting it into slices.

Pancakes

Pancakes are not really Spanish food, but they are very popular in my household. They are bipolar food: guilt-inducing if you eat them and guilt-redeeming if you make them. You have been working late, or travelling for business, you notice how the family starts being a bit grumpy with you, then you announce in the morning that you are making pancakes and that is it, you are back to being 'the best mum in the world' in just 20 minutes. Simply priceless.

They are also really simple to make. You can eat them with lemon juice and sugar as a dessert, or with maple syrup or jam for breakfast. I normally let the children flip the pancakes, which for some reason they really enjoy.

You also need a non-stick pan (preferably very small). If you do not have a small pancake pan then make them in a regular-sized pan, but do not add the baking powder, otherwise you will end up with a cross between an American pancake and a crêpe... not a good mix.

Makes enough for a family at breakfast time

1 glass of plain flour
1 glass of whole or semi-skimmed milk (about 150ml)
1 egg, lightly beaten
1 tsp baking powder (optional, see recipe introduction)
1 tbsp caster sugar
pinch of sea salt
unsalted butter

Mix all the ingredients well except the butter, either by hand or with a hand-held blender. Heat the pan over a medium-high heat (for the choice of pan, see the recipe introduction) with a bit of butter in it, the size of a hazelnut more or less.

When the butter has melted, pour in enough of the pancake mixture to coat the pan. After two or three minutes (when you see bubbles appearing over the surface) flip the pancake over with the help of a spatula, or by flipping it if you dare. Wait for another minute and serve immediately, or keep warm, while you cook the remaining pancakes.

French toast

This is actually called 'lost bread' (*pain perdu*) in French, which seems much more accurate to me than 'French toast'... especially as the French do not seem to make any bread like this. In Spain we make a version of this called *torrijas* which calls for olive oil as opposed to butter and has a sugar syrup (*almíbar*) poured on top, but my children prefer the simpler French version.

With my younger children you get plenty of brownie points in the morning if you make these.

Makes 4–5 slices

1 egg, lightly beaten
200ml whole or semi-skimmed milk
½ tsp vanilla extract
4–5 slices of stale bread
unsalted butter
caster sugar
berries, to serve

Beat the egg, milk and vanilla in a shallow dish. Soak the bread slices in this mixture (do not let them soak for too long).

Put a bit of butter in a frying pan over a medium heat. When the butter has melted, fry the soaked slices until they are golden, turning them so that they become golden on both sides.

When you take them out, sprinkle some sugar on top and serve. You can serve them with all sorts of fruit, but berries work particularly well here.

Churros with chocolate

These are totally addictive heavenly bits of fried dough that we normally eat with thick hot chocolate. My paternal grandmother, Angela, used to prepare these for breakfast on Sundays when we were staying with her.

Churros serve many purposes. They are mostly eaten whenever there is a fair (which in my village is at the end of September on the day of Saint Michael, or in Spanish *San Miguel*, hence the name of my youngest son).

At the other end of the spectrum, posh Spanish ladies have chocolate with *churros* for a snack in the afternoon (*merienda*), just as posh British ladies would have scones with a cream tea. How they all – regardless of nationality – manage to stay thin after all that is beyond me.

Churros are also 'love food': if somebody really loves you they will wake up early and go to buy you some *churros* for breakfast, just as in France they will bring you the more glamorous croissants.

But *churros* really come into their own in the early hours. If you have been partying in Spain (I know… again!) and you come back after 5am – which can happen in the summer more often than you may think as people start having dinner at 10–10.30pm – you make one last stop in the *churrería* for a chocolate with *churros* before you go to bed. There is simply no better way to end a really good party, which is why, at our wedding, Nick and I served them at 7am when the party was – reluctantly! – coming to an end.

To make this, you also need a *churrera*, which is like a hard plastic piping device that you can easily buy online. This is ideal because the dough is very stiff. Alternatively you can pipe these out with a normal piping bag, though the *churros* will not look so nice.

If you cannot find *a la taza* chocolate, just use any good dark chocolate in the same proportion. To help it thicken, you can dissolve ½ tsp cornflour in a little bit of warm milk and add it to the chocolate as you start to stir. This makes a properly thick chocolate, none of the watery stuff that some coffee houses sell nowadays.

Makes enough for 4 (though I can easily eat all these on my own…)

For the churros
1 mug of plain flour
pinch of sea salt
lots of oil (preferably flavourless sunflower,
    but refined olive oil will also do)
caster sugar, to sprinkle

For the chocolate (per person)
1 mug of whole milk
40g chocolate for hot chocolate, of the *a la taza* variety
    (or see recipe introduction)

Make the *churros*: heat one mug of water until it is boiling. Pour the water over the flour and salt in a bowl and mix. Put the dough into a *churrera* or piping bag (see recipe introduction).

Heat the oil in a large saucepan or deep-fat fryer until it is very hot (make sure it only comes one-third of the way up the sides of your chosen pan). Press the *churrera* or piping bag over the oil (with care) in order to fry the dough. As soon as the dough touches the oil, cut it with scissors into sticks of around 15cm. When they are golden, turn the *churros* over with a slotted spoon. (Take care not to crowd the pan.)

When they are golden on both sides, take them out of the pan with the slotted spoon and put them on kitchen paper to blot off the excess oil. Sprinkle with sugar.

Meanwhile, heat the milk over a medium heat. When the milk is warm, add the chocolate, broken into bits. Keep stirring until it begins to boil. You will see that it thickens to the consistency of double cream. As soon as it thickens you can drink it, though you can also leave it at this point and reheat it later. Serve the chocolate with the *churros*.

FRUIT

My grandfather had a real talent with fruit trees. He had a wonderful orchard (not the ornamental type, the real productive variety) and he mastered the art of grafting trees, so he managed to get pear branches into apple trees and plums crossed with cherries. It all looked terribly adventurous and magical to me as a child.

Fruit is also a bit of a teaser in my home as my mother has made it part of her daily fight to convince us all to return to Spain. As we eat an insipid slice of watermelon after lunch in a London summer she will say casually, 'How wonderful is the fruit in Spain, eh, kids?' and, as she serves oranges in the winter to our children, she often comments, 'Oranges from Spain, try them, you just do not have those in the UK.' Obviously the whole cycle of agricultural exports has not registered with her, but who can blame her for trying to get us all back home?

In this chapter you will find lots of recipes to deal with gluts, whether in my middle son's favourite moist apple cake, vats of jam, or a very Spanish *membrillo* (quince paste) that is so good with cheese.

Chevening

Recipes with fallen fruit

The best-known feature of Chevening is its maze, but just beside the maze there is a beautiful orchard. Most years, the fruit was not picked up, something that, as the granddaughter of four farmers, I simply cannot stand. If you have a fruit tree and you are not going to eat the fruit, give it to a neighbour – even to a stranger – but don't let it rot. And, just for the record, that rule applies regardless of whether you are a normal person with a fruit tree in a little garden, or one of the men in red corduroys who often decide how big houses such as Chevening should be run. Wasting fruit is a sin.

These are the things that we have done over the last five years with the unpicked fruit from Chevening:

Apple sauce

You can have this on its own as a winter dessert, with yogurt or cream, or with pork chops… You only need apples and a little bit of water. Do not add sugar.

Peel, core and chop eight cooking or eating apples into big chunks. Put them in a pan with 4–5 tbsp of water. Place over a medium heat, wait until the water boils, then cover with a lid, reduce the heat to its lowest and wait for five to eight minutes. Turn the heat off but keep the lid on for 15 minutes, more or less. If you want a smooth sauce you may want to mix this in a food processor, but we like it with chunks.

Apple jam

This is a wonderful jam. Try it either on toast or with cheese.

Makes as much jam as you have fruit

strong cooking apples (if you are lucky enough to be able
     to get them from the tree, all the better)
juice of ½ lemon per 1kg of fruit
500g granulated sugar per 1kg of fruit

Peel and core the apples and cut them into cubes. Toss them with the lemon juice so that they do not turn brown. Put them in a heavy-based saucepan with the sugar and bring to the boil over a high heat. As soon as it bubbles, reduce the heat to low and cook for around 40 minutes, stirring often with a wooden spoon. When the mixture turns golden and thick enough to feel heavy on the spoon, it is ready (you can test it on frozen saucers – there is a lot of literature on how to do this on the internet – but we never bother and it always comes out right). Let it rest for 10 minutes, then pour into sterilised jars (see below). It keeps for a long time.

To sterilise jars, you can put them through the dishwasher at its highest temperature and then place, open sides down, in an oven preheated to 120°C/250°F/gas mark ½, leaving them in there for 20 minutes. But the very easiest method of all is to wet the jars with water and microwave on a high setting (I use a 700W oven) for two minutes.

Moist apple cake

My middle son loves this cake. It is full of apples so at least, when you cook this, you know you are getting some fruit into him.

Serves 8–10

225g unsalted butter, softened, plus more for the tin
500g cooking apples, or eating apples
finely grated zest and juice of 1 unwaxed lemon
225g caster sugar or light brown soft sugar, plus 3 tbsp more for the topping
225g self-raising flour
2 tsp bicarbonate of soda
3 eggs, lightly beaten
30g ground almonds
3 tbsp icing sugar, to serve

Preheat the oven to 180°C/350°F/gas mark 4. Butter a 25cm cake tin and line the base with baking parchment.

Core the apples, chop them finely and mix them with half the lemon juice so they don't turn brown.

Cream the butter and caster or light brown sugar, by hand or with an electric mixer. Add the lemon zest. Separately mix the flour with the bicarbonate of soda. Then add the eggs to the butter mixture, one at a time, alternating with 3 tbsp of the flour mixture after each addition of egg, until all the flour is in. Finally add the ground almonds and stir in the apples and remaining lemon juice. Sprinkle 2 tbsp more caster or light brown sugar on top and bake for one hour (start checking after 50 minutes).

As with all moist cakes, you need to wait for 10–15 minutes to take the cake out of the tin. Once it is on the serving plate but while it is still warm, sprinkle with the last 1 tbsp of caster or light brown sugar. When it is nearly cold, sift over the icing sugar.

This cake is lovely when it is served warm. My children like it on its own, though it is also very nice with cream or ice cream.

Membrillo (quince paste)

Now this is a recipe well worth remembering, because shop-bought quince paste is absurdly expensive.

Quince comes into season in October. In my village, Olmedo, there are various people with quince trees and they normally give some fruit as presents, so that most of us end up with a couple of kilos of quince paste (if you are really lucky they give it to you already made, normally in square 1kg tins that keep for a month or two).

If you buy quinces when they are in season, just leave them in the kitchen or sitting room for a while, as they have the most wonderful fragrance. Mix the yellow quinces with some pomegranates in a bowl: that is the picture of the Mediterranean autumn, just as a bowl of peaches is the image of the Mediterranean summer.

Eat *membrillo* with hard cheese, on top of cream cheese on toast, or just with bread.

If you keep the water in which you boiled the quinces, add 2 tbsp of sugar per litre and boil it again. Then, when it is cold, dilute it with water or ice and add a handful of mint leaves. If you are adventurous, add a little bit of vodka, too. Very very very good.

Makes 3 small trays

4–5 quinces
granulated sugar
juice of 1 lemon, or to taste

Cut the quinces into chunks (we do not peel or core them). Just cover them with water in a saucepan and bring to the boil, then reduce the heat and simmer until they are soft. Drain off the water (reserve it to make a delicious drink, see recipe introduction) and purée with a hand-held blender or in a food mill (see page 78).

Weigh the puréed quinces and return them to the pan. Add the same weight of sugar. Bring this to the boil and then let it all simmer for 10–15 minutes, stirring very often, until the paste becomes dark brown. Take the pan off the heat and add the juice of a lemon, or to taste. Put in three rectangular plastic boxes or foil trays and let cool completely. It should become solid after one hour or so. Cover with the box lids, or the foil tray covers. This keeps well in the fridge for a couple of months.

Apple paste

This is very similar to *membrillo*, but it has a more delicate taste. My grandmother made this *dulce de manzana* every year with the apples from her farm. She also made her own sheep's milk cheese, that we used to eat with the apple paste.

In fact, being with my gran, helping her to stir a huge bucket of sheep's milk early in the morning, is one of my earliest memories ever. Unfortunately I have lost her recipe for cheese, though even if I had it, I would not be able to make her cheese… she simply had magic hands for it.

> apples (cooking or eating apples are both fine for this)
> juice of ½ lemon per 1kg of fruit
> 750g granulated sugar per 1kg of fruit

Peel and core the apples and cut them into cubes. Toss them with the lemon juice so that they do not turn brown. Put them into a pan with the sugar and boil for around 40 minutes. Start on a high heat and, as soon as it bubbles, reduce to a low heat. Stir it often with a wooden spoon.

When the mixture gets brown, put it into rectangular plastic boxes or foil trays and let it cool down completely. Cover it with the box lids, or with the foil tray covers. If it is properly covered it keeps forever in the fridge. We often made ours in September and it was still great to eat the following August.

Apricot clafoutis

One of the things I value most in my education is that my parents made an effort, within their means, to get us to see how people in other countries live. In turn I myself brainwash my kids about going through the world 'with the antennae on'. I remind them of this so often that now, every time I mention it, they chorus the line with me.

When I was a child, we used to take long car trips to other countries in the summer. They were not luxurious, nor about leisure, we went there to see and learn it all: during the B&B trips we did in the 1980s from Devon to Inverness and back to London and then Kent, I saw more of the UK than I have seen in 10 years of living here!

The last trip we did with my father before he died in a car accident was to the north of Austria, from where we visited the Czech Republic, Hungary and Slovakia (and managed a couple of stops in France as well). We were based in a region where fresh apricots (one of my favourite fruits) were in season and we bought whole boxes of them. After sightseeing each day we used to eat so many apricots that every time I now eat them I cannot help thinking of those happy times with him.

Finding good apricots is hard, so if you do, just eat them on their own. But otherwise, with the regular, imperfect supermarket fruits, you can make this.

Serves 6–8

40g unsalted butter, plus more for the dish
500g fresh apricots
100g caster sugar
40g plain flour
250ml whole or semi-skimmed milk
3 eggs, lightly beaten
icing sugar, to serve

Preheat the oven to 180°C/350°F/gas mark 4. Butter a ceramic or Pyrex oven dish (22cm square is about the right size; just use the dish you have that is closest to that).

Cut the apricots in half, taking the stones out, and arrange them in the dish. Sprinkle them with half the sugar.

Separately whisk the rest of the sugar, the flour, milk and eggs until smooth, then pour this batter on top of the apricots. Cut the 40g of butter into little squares and dot them on top of the clafoutis.

Bake for 40 minutes. Sprinkle with the icing sugar just as you take it out of the oven (you can also grill it now for three or four minutes for a golden finish). Eat promptly.

Plum jam and damson jam

After the 2005 election, we lived in a house in Sheffield that we bought from an elderly couple. In the garden there was a wonderful Victoria plum tree that produced kilos and kilos of fruit.

The house had really good karma… at least until I discovered a mouse in the larder and, given my complete phobia about rodents, left the house and solemnly declared that I wasn't going back. I then returned to my senses (with considerable persuasion from Nick) and went back to the house, but only after calling for a mice exterminator and inflicting serious damage to the rodent population of Sheffield Hallam.

The family of the old lady left many things behind when they sold their house to us. One of them was a huge proper jam pan and more than 100 jam pots. I somehow got it into my head that this was a kind of spiritual inheritance from the old lady to me, and got to making plum jam… I am generally a highly rational person, but even I lose it sometimes. When I say 'I made jam', I really mean 'I Made Jam'. Lots of it. Almost industrial quantities. Certainly enough to provide for all our family and friends. It was in fact on one of those weekend days making jam, surrounded by pots, sterilising equipment and endless boxes of unpitted plums, that I had the equivalent of my midlife crisis. I burst into tears, whingeing that after all the difficult legal cases I handle and all I had studied, I had just ended up making jam. If you are thinking that is spoilt, I should say in my own defence that when something goes wrong making jam it is easy for anybody, no matter how sound of mind, to lose it big time…

Now that I am over midlife (sniff!), I have come to admit that I will always be better at the law and policy than at jam making. But just as really great male lawyers and policy advisers (and many, many others who are not even half as good!) do not apologise for spending their free time playing golf, or watching rugby, I see no reason to have to hide that I like making jam… though just from time to time.

I have written both these recipes using jam sugar. In fact, I prefer them made with regular sugar as it gives a runnier set, but, with jam sugar, the recipe is more reliable.

PLUM JAM

> *Makes 4–5 jars*
>
> 1kg plums
> 1 tbsp lemon juice, or more to taste
> 1kg jam sugar

Wash and halve the plums, pit them and put them into a heavy-based saucepan. Add 100ml of water and the lemon juice. Bring to the boil over a high heat, then reduce the heat to its lowest and cook for 30–40 minutes. Add the sugar and boil for another 20 minutes or so until it reaches setting point. If you have a sugar thermometer (try Lakeland) this just mean waiting until the mixture reaches 220°C (425°F) degrees. It's not rocket science.

Continued overleaf…

Spoon the jam into warm sterilised jars (see page 225). Cover the surface of the jam with a circle of waxed paper (or baking parchment dipped in flavourless oil), seal the jars and store. They last for months.

For damsons, follow the same procedure with the following proportions:

DAMSON JAM

> *Makes about 4 jars*
>
> 1kg damsons
> 115ml orange juice
> finely grated zest of ½ orange
> 780g jam sugar

The main difference is that you need to boil the damsons whole and take the stones out after the damsons are soft. The easiest way to do this is with your hands, but put some plastic gloves on first as otherwise you will burn yourself.

Strawberry mousse

Halfway through the coalition government, we attended the final at Wimbledon at which Andy Murray beat Roger Federer.

I was sitting beside the Mayor of London, Boris Johnson, who kept wanting to talk, and in the next row to us was the Prime Minister. I was told that the woman sitting beside him was '*his* mum'. I am afraid I went through the whole match thinking that '*his* mum' was Murray's mum, when in fact it was the Prime Minister's mum. As I discovered my mistake walking back to the car, we just could not stop laughing thinking that the Mayor must have thought I was plainly bizarre when I kept shushing him every time he criticised Murray, warning him to be careful as 'the mum' could hear us, and saying that 'the mum' seemed a bit cold about her son to me.

Instead, he published an article shortly afterwards, mentioning that I was 'every bit as lovely, clever and funny as she appears' (for which 'thanks, but no thanks'). So, I suppose the lesson is, even if your conversation does not make any sense, just smile constantly and you will be fine… though to be fair the vanity of your interlocutor may play a part in it as well.

This is a nice strawberry dessert at a fraction of the price of humungously expensive Wimbledon strawberries.

Serves 4–6

350g strawberries
5 leaves of gelatine
125ml double cream
125ml single cream
2 egg whites
70g caster sugar

Blend the strawberries in a food processor or with a hand-held blender. Soak the gelatine in water for 10 minutes, then squeeze out the water. Put the gelatine in a cup with 2 tbsp of fresh water. Microwave on a high setting for 15 seconds (I use a 700W oven). Mix into the berries.

In a separate bowl, combine the two types of cream and beat until you get soft peaks. Fold in the strawberry mixture, taking care not to knock out any air.

In another bowl, beat the egg whites until they form soft peaks. Then beat in the sugar, a spoonful at a time, until they become glossy. Fold this into the mousse, taking care not to lose the air. Spoon into glasses and refrigerate for at least two hours.

You can make this a day in advance, but remember that it contains raw egg, so do not keep it in the fridge for more than 48 hours and bear in mind that the usual restrictions apply (see overleaf).

Yogurt mousse with cherries

In 2011 the US state visit took place. It was such a treat to be able to meet President Obama and his wife. Having seen, during the many years when I was dealing with foreign policy, how much damage US Presidents can do, we should all have given thanks every day when we woke up that the Presidency of the most powerful country in the world was in the hands of such a decent, rational and honest man.

The then-American ambassador hosted a dinner for them, where he not only served treacle tart, but spoke to me about every tiny detail of how you make treacle tart for at least a good half hour.

The current, and sensible, and clever, and just wonderful ambassador – who in addition cooks very well – makes a version of this mousse sometimes for guests.

As with all recipes containing raw eggs, this should not be served to the elderly, pregnant women, babies and toddlers, those with weakened immune systems, or anyone who is already unwell.

Serves 4–6

For the mousse
5 leaves of gelatine
110g double cream
110g single cream
300g Greek yogurt (non-fat if you
    want a 'kind on the figure' version)
50g caster sugar
finely grated zest of
    1 unwaxed lemon
1 egg white

For the compote
200g cherries, fresh or canned
100g caster sugar
1 tbsp lemon juice
3 tbsp brandy or whisky (optional, but it
    is much better with it!)

Put the gelatine in a bowl of cold water so that it softens. Beat the two creams together until you get a ribbony consistency. Mix the yogurt, cream, sugar and lemon zest.

Meanwhile, squeeze the water out of the gelatine and put it in a cup with 2 tbsp of fresh water. Microwave for 15 seconds on a high setting (I use a 700W oven). When this is cold, mix it with the cream.

Beat the egg white until it forms soft peaks, then carefully fold it into the cream.

Separately put the cherries with 40ml of water in a saucepan over a medium heat for 15 minutes. Then add the sugar and lemon juice (and the brandy or whisky if using) and let it simmer for another 15 minutes. Let this cool down completely.

Put 3 tbsp of the compote into each glass. Top with the whipped mousse. Chill in the fridge overnight.

Lemon posset

I love lemons, so I love posset, a simply outstanding British invention that I often serve at dinners. Given that we have so many lemons in Spain, it's a bit of a mystery why we didn't come up with this… thank goodness the British did.

Most recipes call for double cream, but we make this with single cream and it is lighter and nicer. If you prefer the more filling version, use half double and half single cream instead.

Serves 4–6

500ml single cream (or see recipe introduction)
150g caster sugar
85ml lemon juice, and some finely grated unwaxed lemon zest, if you wish

Put the cream and sugar in a saucepan, stir it a few times and bring it to the boil. Reduce the heat and let it simmer for three minutes while you stir it regularly.

Take it off the heat, add the lemon juice (and zest if using) and let it cool down. Pour it into glasses or cups, cover and refrigerate it overnight.

Orange and pomegranate pavlova

The first Foreign Secretary of the coalition government once organised a birthday party at Chevening and, as a result, many of his Party colleagues went there. It was after this that somebody who was at that party (and from that Party) mentioned to us: 'The other government houses are the kind of place that you can imagine your friends owning, but Chevening is properly grand. You know what I mean?' I am not sure I know what the person meant... but what I do know is that clearly I have the wrong kind of friends!

In any case, this is a 'grand' dessert with a Spanish fruit twist.

If you are really into sweet flavours, you can caramelise the oranges first: cut the oranges in slices. Make a caramel by mixing 250g of caster sugar and 125ml of water in a saucepan over a medium heat, while swirling it (not stirring) until the caramel becomes lightly golden. Put the oranges into the pan to coat them in caramel. Without wasting any time, put them on a flat dish and wait for them to get cold.

You can also make this meringue mixture into mini pavlovas; bake those for just 23–25 minutes and leave them in the oven with the door ajar for 50–60 minutes.

Serves 6–8

4 egg whites
pinch of sea salt
250g caster sugar
1 tsp cornflour
1 tsp white wine vinegar
250ml double cream
3 oranges
handful of pomegranate seeds
4 mint leaves

Preheat the oven to 180°C/350°F/gas mark 4.

Beat the egg whites with the salt for a few minutes, with an electric mixer or by hand, until they form stiff peaks. Beat in the sugar, 1 tbsp at a time. Sprinkle the cornflour and vinegar on top and fold them carefully into the egg whites. Draw a 25cm circle on a piece of baking parchment and pile up the mixture on top of it, building up the edges to form a slight rim.

As you put the meringue in the oven, reduce the oven temperature to 150°C/300°F/gas mark 2. After one and a half hours, turn off the oven, prop the door open with the handle of a wooden spoon and let it cool completely (preferably overnight).

Put the meringue pavlova on to a plate. Whip the cream to soft peaks and pile it on top. Cut the oranges into squares (carefully removing all pith and seeds) and arrange them on top of the cream. Scatter the pomegranate seeds on top of the oranges and decorate with the mint leaves.

Lemonade (and pink lemonade)

There is normally one day every year – one of those rare sunny days – when the children ask me to make lemonade. The conversation goes something like this: 'Why don't WE do something to earn some pocket money?' 'What about selling the neighbours lemonade?' This is normally followed by:

'Mama, can YOU make lemonade that we can sell?'

'Can YOU buy the ice?'

'And would YOU set up the table?'

'Would YOU mind writing the prices on a large piece of paper?'

'Oh wait, would YOU give us change?'

I suppose the only positive thing to come from this is that as 'THEY' pocket the money while 'YOU' do all the work, they learn about capitalism in its purest form. But in truth this is not hard to make.

Makes about 1½ litres

6 unwaxed lemons
100g caster sugar
pinch of salt
handful of ice

Quarter the lemons and finely pare off the zest, leaving all the white pith behind. Now, with a sharp knife, scoop out the lemon flesh, to leave a shell of pith. Discard the pith.

Put the lemon zest and flesh in a blender with the sugar and salt, pouring in one litre of water, then blend until smooth. Strain the lemonade through a sieve. This tastes even better if you can now let it rest overnight.

When you're ready to drink it (or sell it), add the ice.

And if you want to make pink lemonade, follow the same recipe but use only 85g caster sugar and add a handful of strawberries to the blender.

Pineapple and mint salad

This is a super-simple dessert that I often serve at dinner parties. It never ever fails to please. The secret ingredient is the vodka. It always keeps the conversation going…

Serve it with chocolate brownies; everybody loves it.

Serves 6

1 pineapple, peeled and cored
handful of mint leaves
2 tbsp caster sugar
1 (or 2… or 3!) tbsp vodka, really depending on your mood,
    and whether or not you are bored with the conversation

Cut the pineapple into small chunks.

Just before you are going to serve it, put the mint leaves and sugar into a mortar and bash them with the pestle (do this at the last minute as otherwise the mint will turn brown). Stir in the vodka. Mix the contents of the mortar with the pineapple and serve.

DESSERTS
AND BAKING

I hope I do not get a massive national bashing for saying this, but we are actually not too good at desserts in Spain… and certainly much worse at baking than the UK! Part of the explanation for this is that Spanish cooking is a bit of an everyday cultural experiment: add a bit of this, a pinch of that, replace this ingredient with whatever you have at hand… while baking requires a precise attitude to all ingredients and an instinctive rigour with the quantities that most of us Spanish cooks lack.

I myself got into baking in my thirties as soon as I understood that experimenting with the quantities was a no-no. While I like baking and have developed a good hand at it, I am in truth more salty than sweet (in every way!) and would go for a plate of Ibérico ham over cake any day.

But even those of you that, like me, do not have much of a sweet tooth will find it hard to resist some of these dessert recipes – that take me back to my childhood – and some of the cakes that have become part of my family's cooking repertoire. Two of my children, who like sugary things, very much agree.

Leche frita

Leche frita means 'fried milk'; in fact this is fried thick custard. Though it is typical in most of the northern half of Spain, my mother, who considers this one of her specialities, claims that the best is from Palencia, where she comes from. She makes a very good *leche frita*, mostly because she makes it thicker than they normally serve it in restaurants. Pretty much every Spaniard – me included – believes that when it comes to custard, this is 'The' dessert. Much, much better than crème brûlée. You may feel like you want to add more flour to get this to set, though if you do, please remember that it is supposed to be creamy, not thick and floury, so don't add too much!

We not only fry custard in Spain, but all sorts of things: if we want to send somebody to hell we ask them to go to 'fry asparagus' or 'fry black puddings'; and if somebody keeps bothering us we say that they are trying to 'fry our brain'. I can think of a good number of people who regularly fry my brain and that I would like to send to fry asparagus instead!

The best way to serve this is with vanilla or *turrón* (nougat) ice cream on the side.

Makes 20 squares / Serves 10 (or 8... or 5... it just depends on how greedy you are!)

1 litre whole milk
5 egg yolks, plus 2 eggs, lightly beaten
5 heaped tbsp caster sugar
5 heaped tbsp plain flour, plus more to dust
strip of unwaxed lemon zest (without the pith; around the size of a small finger)
sunflower oil, to fry

Put the milk in a pan over a really low heat. Separately mix the 5 egg yolks and the sugar, add them to the milk, then whisk in the flour and finally the strip of lemon zest. Now start stirring, in a clockwise direction, constantly until the mixture thickens. Do not increase the heat, as the key to this dish is that the mixture thickens slowly and it does not burn. You need to wait until you get the first bubbles, by which time the mixture will thicken so that when you stir you should be able to see the bottom of the pan in the spoon's wake. This should take 10–15 minutes.

Transfer the cream to a flat tray (not too big, so that you get thick squares afterwards. Just as a guide, we do this in two normal size dishes). Let it cool down for a couple of hours.

When it is totally cold, cut the cream into squares. Put the flour and whole eggs in two separate dishes. Coat the squares of cream first with flour and then with egg.

Pour the sunflower oil into a deep small pan (the oil should not come more than halfway up the sides) and place over a medium heat. Fry the squares of cream, turning once, until they are golden on both sides. This should normally take a couple of minutes on each side.

Eat while still warm.

Chocolate olive oil mousse

The day the coalition was formed, I set up two conditions. Just two: that I would keep on working (not really a condition, more a matter of fact); and that we would continue living in our house.

The following day the Powers That Be asked Nick to visit a posh apartment at Admiralty Arch and asked him to try to persuade me to reconsider. My 'reconsideration' went something like: 'Let me think about it... mmm... no way...!'

In exchange – or probably in revenge – for my far-too-quick reconsideration, they insisted on installing a top-of-the-range sophisticated (and mostly unnecessary) security system throughout our house: they drilled plenty of holes, mounted cameras and panic buttons, set up a complex code system, even put in a red telephone that we were told, if it was used, would lead to a helicopter flying to our home in a matter of minutes (try telling that to three boys under nine without them wanting to pick up that red phone all the time!). Even I was impressed, and I am generally the cynical sort.

It took just two weeks for one of us (yes, that one!) to close a window badly and activate the alarm. We prepared to face the embarrassment of having to admit a silly error in front of a massive police display. We waited for five minutes, 10, 15, 20... but no helicopters, no police cars, no alarms, not a smidgen of a sound...

Half an hour later we got a call from my father-in-law, who was placidly sitting in a local café in France. He had received a call from our old alarm company asking if there was a problem in our house. After all that palaver, those very clever Powers That Be had forgotten to connect the super-duper security system to the police.

My father-in-law – who is one of the best people to cook for as he likes every bit of food you make for him – is a real chocolate lover, so this is a chocolate mousse recipe with a Spanish twist. Unless you are an olive oil addict it is better to avoid virgin olive oil for this, as the taste is very strong.

Makes 6

150g dark chocolate, broken into pieces	80ml refined olive oil
	60g caster sugar
4 large eggs, separated	a little Maldon salt

Melt the chocolate in the microwave or in a heatproof bowl over simmering water (don't let the bowl touch the water). Once it has melted, let it cool down a little. Add the egg yolks and whisk it all well. It will become a very thick paste. Then pour in the olive oil slowly, while you continue to whisk.

Separately whisk the egg whites until they form soft peaks. Gradually add the sugar, 1 tbsp at a time, whisking all the time until the mixture becomes glossy. Beat one-third of the egg whites with the chocolate, then fold in the remaining egg whites carefully.

Pour into glasses or ramekins and chill for three hours. Sprinkle a little Maldon salt over to serve. You can also shape the mousse into quenelles with two spoons warmed under a hot tap and serve it with Olive oil cake (see page 266) and an orange salad.

Poshed-up yogurt

One of the good things about being close to the British government is that you can learn how most in the 'ruling class' live. By and large, they pretend that the fuss normally associated with trying to climb the social ladder does not affect them a tiny little bit. That is why they prefer clothes with holes in them rather than brand names and favour 'lovely little cottages' over five-star hotels. Everything to do with what you achieve is 'natural': you are naturally sporting, naturally talented, a natural linguist… it never seems to cross their minds that effort might have had anything to do with it.

When it comes to food, though, there is always room for a bit of poshing up. This is easy. Try pea purée: mush some peas, mix them with crème fraîche, spread them over toasted slices of baguette and sprinkle with chopped mint. Or get a bowl of houmous, drizzle olive oil and harissa on top and tear up a little bit of sourdough to go with it.

This is a favourite of mine: poshing up Greek yogurt to make a really nice dessert.

Makes as big a bowl as you need

Greek yogurt
pomegranate seeds
walnuts, pecan nuts or hazelnuts, toasted if you like
honey
a few mint leaves

Put the Greek yogurt into a serving dish. Scatter the pomegranate seeds and nuts on top. Drizzle with the honey and decorate with the mint leaves.

My family at a celebration, eating flan

Flan

Most Spanish mums know how to make a flan, or at least they did when I was little. This is one of those dishes prone to kitchen disasters: the caramel gets too dark, or it is too light; the flan has holes; it sticks to the pan; it collapses as you take it out… but follow this recipe faithfully and you'll get a proper flan. It is so central to Spanish home cooking that, when somebody makes consistently good flans, they escalate in the ladder of good cooks to a different level. You can hear Spaniards talking about the 'flans of their mothers' with the same admiration as if they were works of art.

Flan is one of those recipes that requires a certain self-confidence. If you start out having doubts as to whether the flan will turn out well, it is very likely that you'll end up with a bad flan. If you need a little technical help, put some egg shells or a spoon in the water of the bain-marie when you put the flans into the oven. This prevents the water from boiling and, as a result, the flan will cook slowly and be consistently perfect. As in life, self-confidence in flan-making is something you can learn…

We use small metal pudding basins, but you can cook them in regular ramekins, or make a big flan in a large pudding basin or Pyrex bowl.

Makes 6 small flans

For the caramel
75g caster sugar

For the flan
500ml whole milk
3 eggs, plus 2 egg yolks
175g caster sugar
½ tbsp vanilla extract

Preheat the oven to 150°C/300°F/gas mark 2.

For the caramel, put the sugar in a saucepan with 6 tbsp of water. Place over a medium heat. Let it bubble without touching it (do not stir) until it becomes a dark golden colour. It takes three or four minutes only, but you have to watch it carefully as it is easy to burn it. Pour the caramel into six metal pudding basins or ramekins and swirl so that it covers their bases.

For the flan, heat the milk until it is about to boil. Separately, in a bowl, mix the eggs, egg yolks and sugar and beat well. Add the hot milk, whisking constantly, and finally add the vanilla. Pour the mixture into the pudding basins or ramekins on top of the caramel. Boil a kettle.

Put the basins in a deep oven tray and on to a shelf of the preheated oven. Now – carefully – pour boiling water into the tray, up to one-third of the height of the ramekins, to form a bain marie. Slide in the oven shelf and shut the oven door.

The small flans are ready in 30 minutes. If you make a big flan with all the mixture, it will need 50 minutes to cook.

Let the flans cool down for at least two hours. With a sharp knife, go around the edge of each basin, then turn them out on to plates. If you keep them inside their basins or ramekins, they will keep for two or three days in the fridge.

Flavoured milk ice cream

The Mediterranean coast of Spain – particularly Valencia and Alicante – is famous for its ice creams. Most Spanish people of my generation have a particularly affinity with Alicante as, during the transition to democracy, when our families were able to afford going on holiday 'to the sea' for the first time, we went there. Roads were terrible, so these were massive trips: more than 12 hours in small cars with all the children packed in the back seat (all after the arguments between the parents about the amount of luggage, and without any seat belts of course). We used to go to huge towers of packed flats that we rented for a month, and though the holidays were not luxurious by any means, we simply loved it there. In the evenings we were allowed an ice cream: *leche merengada* (flavoured milk) was my favourite.

This recipe contains raw eggs so, as ever, the usual warnings apply (see page 236).

Makes about 1.2 litres

1 litre whole milk	100ml double cream
finely grated zest of 1 unwaxed lemon	4 egg whites
1 cinnamon stick	a little ground cinnamon
70g caster sugar	

Boil the milk, lemon zest and cinnamon stick with 40g of the sugar. As soon as it boils, take it off the heat and let it cool down. If you put this into the fridge and drink it when it is very cold it is called *leche merengada* (literally 'meringued milk'). Add the cream to the milk.

Separately whisk the 4 egg whites with the remaining 30g of sugar as if you are going to prepare a meringue (see page 238). Fold this into the milk mixture carefully, so that you do not lose the air. Pour it into an ice cream machine (or into a tray in the freezer and whisk it with a fork three or four times, every 90 minutes or so). When you are going to serve it, sprinkle a bit of ground cinnamon on top.

Me with my brother, sister and cousins on holiday in a big block of flats in Alicante

Rice pudding *Arroz con leche*

Lots of countries have a version of rice pudding. In Spain, the best rice pudding (*arroz con leche*) comes from the North, notably from Asturias, where they have wonderful milk. Good *arroz con leche* should be creamy, silky and not dry. Watching an old lady from Asturias prepare this is an experience in itself: they keep stirring and talking over it for at least an hour.

The recipe below is a more modern and therefore less laborious one. Not as good as the real thing, but very good nevertheless.

Serves 4–6

> 200g short-grain rice, such as Bomba or Arborio
> 1 litre whole milk, plus about 350ml more
> 1 cinnamon stick
> finely grated zest of 1 unwaxed lemon
> 125g caster sugar
> a very little ground cinnamon (optional)

Wash the rice thoroughly. In a pan heat the 1 litre of milk, the cinnamon stick and lemon zest until the milk boils. As soon as you see the bubbles, add the rice. Reduce the heat to its lowest and let it simmer for 20 minutes, stirring it often from the moment you put in the rice, as otherwise it will stick to the pan.

Add the sugar and simmer for another 25 minutes. During this last 25 minutes, keep adding a little more milk every time you stir it, especially if the mixture is starting to stick to the pan (we use 350ml because the children like it creamy, but you may be able to do it with less milk). Put it into small bowls and let it set for at least 30 minutes.

We serve it with a bit of cinnamon (very little) sprinkled on top. You can also cover it with sugar and caramelise it with a kitchen blowtorch (this is how they do it in Asturias). You can keep this, covered, in the fridge for a couple of days; take it out of the fridge for 30 minutes or so before serving.

Elephant ears

Nick, like me, is not normally into sweet foods, but whether they are shop-bought or home-made, he finds it hard to say no to these. They are a good example of the differences between nationalities: while the Spanish and French see this shape as palm trees (*palmeras* or *palmiers*), the British see them as 'elephant ears', and the Germans as pig's ears (*schweineohren*)! They taste great, which at the end of the day – no matter what names or nationalities – is the only thing that counts.

Makes 8–10

> 1 sheet of ready-rolled (preferably all-butter) puff pastry
> 5–6 handfuls of caster sugar

Unfurl the puff pastry rectangle. Sprinkle a generous amount of sugar on top of it. Press a little with a rolling pin so that the sugar sticks to the pastry. Fold the pastry by bringing the longest sides towards the centre so that both longest sides meet right in the middle of your rectangle. You should end up with a narrower rectangle.

Sprinkle more sugar on it. Press down again with the rolling pin. Fold it again by bringing both extreme (short) sides towards the centre.

Sprinkle again with some sugar. Press down with the rolling pin and fold again, then finally roll into a cylinder. Wrap it in cling film and refrigerate for 20 minutes.

Meanwhile, preheat the oven to 200°C/400°F/gas mark 6. Take the pastry out of the fridge and cut little slices off the cylinder. Put them on a baking tray and flatten them a bit with a spatula.

Bake for 20 minutes, turning after 12 minutes so that they get golden on both sides.

Scones

I love scones. I discovered them when I first came to the UK with my family and we stayed for three weeks in Devon. It rained constantly for every single day of those three weeks and when we could not cope with the rain any longer we would go to a tea house for the wonderful Devon scones with cream. I must have put on at least five kilos in those three weeks!

The other place that always reminds me of scones is Chevening, a truly stunning house. Though most of those who run it day-to-day are really generous and professional people, the management of the place is stuck in the 19th century, especially when it comes to children. The first time I went there, with one of Nick's aides, the ex-army officer who ran the house at the time asked me during the first five minutes of our encounter – and with a straight face – 'Do you have a nanny?' I naïvely responded, 'Yes,' only to realise shortly afterwards that the purpose of the question was to suggest that the nanny would be at all times with the children in what he called 'A spare room that we can arrange in the other wing of the house'.

I suppose, in his understanding, this would happen while Nick and I attended to the more important matters of life. I further presume that for him these were: drinking tea with scones; taking a cold sherry before dinner; discussing the latest society gossip; and reading the *Daily Mail* (not necessarily in that order). You would need not just an ex-army man, but a whole fully functioning army to get me to behave like that!

Serves 4–6

225g self-raising flour, plus more to dust
pinch of sea salt
75g unsalted butter, chopped, at room temperature, plus more for the tray
50g caster sugar
1 egg, lightly beaten
1 tbsp milk
1 tbsp plain yogurt, plus more to brush

Preheat the oven to 220°C/425°F/gas mark 7. Sift the flour and salt into a bowl. Add the butter and rub it in with your fingers until the whole thing looks like breadcrumbs. Stir in the sugar. Beat the egg, milk and yogurt together and add it to the mixture. Mix it all with a knife and then, at the end, with your fingers (very lightly). Roll the dough out on a lightly floured surface into a 3cm-thick circle and cut out the scones with a cutter. The scones should look tall and thick.

Put them on a buttered baking tray (we used a silicone tray from Lakeland) and brush a bit of yogurt on top. Sprinkle a tiny bit of flour over the scones and bake for 10–15 minutes. Serve with cream and strawberry jam.

Nun's sighs

When Prince George, the new heir to the throne, was born, we sent a big packet of coffee and a cover embroidered by the nuns at my village. The nuns are very poor and they live by selling their hand-made embroidery, eating the charity food that others give them. In Spain there is a tradition to bring eggs to the nuns on your wedding day so that their praying stops the rain, which means they end up with many eggs. (Obviously the prayers for good weather have more chance of working in Spain than in the UK.) With the eggs they bake biscuits and cakes, which they sell afterwards.

This is a typical treat made by Spanish nuns. They are very light, as light as the sigh of a nun, hence their name. You will need paper fairy cake cases.

Makes about 14

3 egg whites
125g caster sugar
125g ground almonds
finely grated zest of ½ unwaxed lemon

Preheat the oven to 220°C/425°F/gas mark 7.

Whisk the egg whites until stiff. Add the sugar 1 tbsp at a time, while continuing to whisk, until the mixture becomes glossy. Fold in the almonds and then the lemon zest.

Spoon into paper fairy cake cases. Bake until golden; they take 10–12 minutes, but it depends a bit on the size of the paper cases.

Cat's tongues

Six times I tried and five times I failed to bake these biscuits when the Prime Minister and his wife came for dinner at our house. The first batch burned; the second stuck to the silicone mat; the third I baked on foil but they got stuck again. The fourth batch were undercooked; the fifth batch expanded and I could not separate them… and the last lot was finally edible, but only just. My bad mood multiplied every time by a ratio of about five. As the time of the dinner approached, my eldest son unhelpfully whispered in my ear, 'Should I go to the corner shop to buy biscuits?' That is what I call a lack of faith.

These are in fact very easy and go well with lemon posset or other creamy desserts (they are also lighter than shortbread).

Makes enough for 4–6

125g unsalted butter
125g caster sugar
125g plain flour
1 egg, lightly beaten
2 tbsp milk
½ tsp vanilla extract (optional)

Preheat the oven to 180°C/350°F/gas mark 4. Cover a couple of baking trays with baking parchment, or use silicone mats.

Melt the butter. Add the sugar, flour, egg, milk and vanilla, in that order. Mix it all well with a wooden spoon.

Make 7–8cm long lines with the mixture (you can either use a piping bag or a teaspoon). Bake in the oven for 10 minutes. As soon as you see that the edges are turning golden, take them out of the oven. Let them cool down on a wire rack before you attempt to move them from the baking parchment or silicone mat.

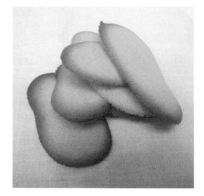

My Aunt Charo

Snowy mountain

My Aunt Charo died when I was eight. It was my first encounter with death and it was all the more tragic because she was only 46. With her thick dark hair and green eyes, I romantically remember her as one of the most beautiful women I have ever met. When she was young, if she had been side by side with Ava Gardner, you would have seriously struggled to decide which was the most elegant, or so my family says! Whether true or not, the fact is that she had endless men after her… and probably because of that she did not marry any of them.

Once she was asked to be a godmother at a wedding in my grandparents' village, the wedding of the daughter of the shepherd. At that time, weddings were celebrated with a banquet in the fields and godmothers had to pay for or prepare all of it. (In Spain, we have godmothers both at christenings and weddings. In fact the godmother can be as important as the bride, as they are often the mother of the groom.) For the wedding's dessert, Aunt Charo made this… and the whole village was so impressed that the elders of the village still remember the occasion even today.

This dessert is really a better version of the French *îles flottantes* (a dessert that I normally find heavy and a bit 'in your face'). Instead, this is light, subtle and elegant.

Serves 8

4 eggs, separated
4 tbsp caster sugar
1 tbsp cornflour (optional)
800ml whole milk
a very little ground cinnamon

Whisk the egg whites until you get stiff peaks. Separately mix the yolks, sugar and the cornflour (if using; the 'proper' recipe does not use cornflour, but then you have to be very careful as it might split).

In a broad sauté pan, heat half the milk until it boils. Reduce the heat to its lowest. As soon as you see the bubbles get big, take a spoonful of the whisked whites and put them one at a time in the milk. Wait for 15 seconds, then turn the blob of meringue over, wait for another 10 seconds, then remove it with a slotted spoon. Shake off any moisture and put it in a serving dish (you may want to use kitchen paper if you get too much milk on the serving dish when you do this).

Once you have cooked all the egg whites (and with the heat still low), add the rest of the milk to the pan, and start pouring the yolk and sugar mixture into the milk little by little (in a thin stream, as for mayonnaise). Keep stirring, always in a clockwise direction, while you do this, until you see the first bubbles. When you do, take the pan off the heat and keep stirring for another three or four minutes. The mixture should be like a really thin custard (coating the back of a spoon, but only just).

Pour the custard on the egg whites carefully (without covering them fully) and sprinkle a little bit of cinnamon on top (only a tiny bit). Sinful.

Lemon curd muffins

I have developed a phobia about cupcakes. For many years I have been a polite, mostly rational, largely civilised, generally generous person… except when it comes to cupcakes. For those many years – all the primary school years of my eldest children – if you whispered into my ears the word 'baking day', the little girl of *The Exorcist* would come out of my body and start baking cupcakes not only competitively but with real fury. Because I knew, I knew (and yes, I did know because I had done it myself) that the world's judgement of me as a mother relied on the icing of those cupcakes.

But then I became class rep a couple of years ago and I realised that after all that effort we actually lose money when we run a baking day. So when I feel like baking, I now try muffins instead.

These are actually delicious for breakfast or tea, as the lemon curd bubbles a bit out of the muffins and gives them a nice twist.

As with any baking, the kids love helping with these… and eating them afterwards.

Makes 12

> 250g self-raising flour
> 25g ground almonds (if you do not have this at hand,
>   replace it with 30g more self-raising flour)
> ¾ tsp bicarbonate of soda
> 1 tsp baking powder
> finely grated zest and juice of 1 unwaxed lemon
> 60g caster sugar
> 75g unsalted butter, melted
> 1 egg, lightly beaten
> 100ml whole or semi-skimmed milk
> 1 jar of good-quality shop-bought lemon curd

Preheat the oven to 200°C/400°F/gas mark 6.

Mix the flour, ground almonds, bicarb, baking powder, lemon zest and sugar in a large bowl. Make a well in the centre.

Separately mix the butter, lemon juice, egg and milk. Pour this into the well in the dry ingredients and stir them lightly (ideally just with a fork) to make a batter.

Spoon half the batter into paper muffin cases and place in a cupcake tin, filling them to one-third full for now. Add 1 tsp lemon curd to each, then spoon the remaining batter over to (almost) fill the cases.

Bake for 15–20 minutes until the muffins are golden and risen.

Olive oil cake

Spain is a rather divided country, but if there is something that unites us all, it is our love for olive oil. We are crazy about it. I am afraid we rather look down on butter, margarine and any of the fancy oils that have got into fashion nowadays. We occasionally use sunflower oil when absolutely necessary, but otherwise we use olive oil for everything: from frying, to breakfast – pouring it over bread and sprinkling it with sugar – to getting rid of make up (just try it, it is very good), or making cakes.

Eat this cake on its own with a cup of strong coffee, or as a dessert with a nice orange salad, or with Chocolate olive oil mousse (see page 249).

Makes 1 loaf

unsalted butter, for the tin
4 eggs
175g caster sugar
150ml olive oil
finely grated zest of 1½ unwaxed lemons, or 1 orange if you prefer
170g plain flour
pinch of sea salt
1 tbsp baking powder
3 tbsp pine nuts

Preheat the oven to 180°C/350°F/gas mark 4. Butter a large loaf tin. (Try a tin with about 1-litre capacity; the cake for the photo was baked in a 22 × 12cm tin.)

Mix the eggs and sugar with an electric mixer or by hand until the mixture looks pale. Very gradually pour in the olive oil while you continue mixing, adding it in little bits, or the mixture could curdle. Add the grated lemon zest.

Combine the flour, salt and baking powder and sift it on to the mixture. Fold it in carefully so that you do not lose the air in the batter. Put it into the prepared tin. It will only about half-fill the tin, but it expands a lot. Sprinkle the pine nuts evenly on top and let it bake in the oven for 40–45 minutes.

Hojuelas

This is a traditional Easter dessert in Spain. One of my aunts (not the *croquetas* aunts!) used to make endless trays of these each Easter (which has a lot of merit, as you need a considerable amount of patience to make them).

They are meant to be as thin as paper and they should break into little pieces when you eat them.

Makes around 18 (if they are as thin as they should be!)

1 egg
½ egg shell of sunflower oil
½ egg shell of tequila, sambuca or vodka (in Spain we use *orujo*
   but that is difficult to find in the UK)
¼ tsp red wine vinegar
pinch of sea salt
1 tbsp caster sugar, plus lots more to serve
125g plain flour
lots of olive oil (refined, not virgin), to fry

Mix the egg, sunflower oil, tequila (or other alcohol) and vinegar and beat well. Then add the salt, the 1 tbsp of sugar and finally the flour. Let it rest for 30 minutes.

Heat the olive oil in a frying pan over a medium-high heat.

Get little balls of the dough, each the size of a walnut. Put the dough balls between two pieces of baking parchment and roll them out as thinly as possible with a rolling pin. When you think they are thin enough, just roll them out a bit more! Take the upper bit of paper off and peel off the pastry carefully. Put the pastry into the olive oil and fry it until each *hojuela* becomes golden. This takes only one minute or so on each side, and you need to turn them over with a slotted spoon, which is very easy as they harden almost immediately.

Remember that the oil should be very hot and you should get big bubbles in each *hojuela* as soon as they touch the hot oil.

When they are golden, take the *hojuelas* out of the pan with a slotted spoon, put them on kitchen paper to blot off the excess oil and sprinkle them with sugar immediately. Naturally, the more sugar you use, the better they taste.

Milk buns *Bollo de leche*

Children love these, either on their own or with butter, jam, cream cheese, ham, cheese… In Spain they are called *bollo de leche* and they are often eaten with a few squares of milk chocolate.

You can make these with plain flour but, if you do so, increase the amount of flour to 550g. It will be a very soft and sticky dough, so handling it requires patience…

It takes a while to prepare these but, to be fair, most of the time is just waiting for them to rise while you get on with other things. ('Homework?' you ask… 'A Fifa game!' they respond…). The good thing about these, though, is that they really give you enough time to have an argument over homework and make up again.

Makes 10

250ml whole or semi-skimmed milk
7g fast-action dried yeast
500g strong bread flour, plus more to dust
2 eggs, lightly beaten, plus 1 more to glaze
110g caster sugar
1 tsp sea salt
100g unsalted butter, at room temperature, in little pieces
a little sunflower oil

Warm 100ml of the milk. Mix the yeast, 50g of the flour and the warm milk and let it rest for 30 minutes until it gets frothy.

Then mix this with the remaining milk and flour, the 2 eggs, sugar and salt. The easiest way to do this is in a food processor fitted with the dough hook for eight to 10 minutes. Add the butter and continue to knead for three or four minutes. Finally, knead by hand on a well-floured surface. This is a very soft dough, so dust your hands well with flour as it is very sticky.

Put the dough into a glass bowl oiled with a tiny bit of sunflower oil and let it rest for two hours until it has doubled in size.

Punch the dough to get rid of the air. Then divide it into 10 parts. Shape each one like a ball, or give them an oval shape. You can also shape them: put the oval shape in front of you and make three 10cm cuts on one of the shortest edges. Roll the oval over itself, starting rolling on the non-cut side, so that when you finish rolling it the cut strips fall over the roll like a blanket.

Put them on one or two baking trays lined with baking parchment. Cover with cling film and wait for another 45 minutes until they rise again.

Preheat the oven to 200°C/400°F/gas mark 6. Brush the buns with the beaten egg. Put them into the oven and bake for 13–15 minutes. Cool on a wire rack.

Index

A

ajoarriero 80
almejas a la marinera 114
almonds: lemon curd muffins 264
    moist apple cake 226
    nun's sighs 259
    romesco sauce 83
apples: apple jam 225
    apple paste 230
    apple sauce 224
    chicken with apple 144
    moist apple cake 226
apricot clafoutis 231
arroz a la cubana 180
arroz con leche 255
aubergines: aubergines with honey 87
    aubergines with *salmorejo* 210
    pasta bake 185
avocados: guacamole 208

B

bacon: easy pasta with bacon
      and peas 182
    migas 205
Basque cod 123
beans: with *ajoarriero* 80
    bean quesadillas 209
    beans with clams 190–1
    see also chickpeas
beef: *bolitas* soup 32
    grilled steak 160
    meatballs 186–7
    Russian steaks 152–3
    San Jacobos 163
bread: easy Mediterranean salad 96
    French toast 219
    migas 205
    romesco sauce 83
    salmorejo 39

buns: milk buns 270
butternut squash: roast chicken
    147
    Thai chickpeas 181
    winter salad 99

C

cakes: moist apple cake 226
    olive oil cake 266
calamares en su tinta 119
camarones: tortillitas de camarones
    61
carrots: carrot salad 94
    garden soup 26
cat's tongues 261
chard with ham 88
cheese: cheese biscuits 216
    chickpea salad 84
    ham and cheese roll 212
    pasta bake 185
    San Jacobos 163
    tomato and cheese loaf 217
    winter salad 99
cherries: yogurt mousse with cherries
    236
chicken: *bolitas* soup 32
    chicken with apple 144
    chicken with garlic 146
    leftover chicken pie 192
    roast chicken three ways
      147–8
chickpeas: *bolitas* soup 32
    chickpea salad 84
    fried chickpeas 215
    Lent chickpeas 36
    Thai chickpeas 181
chocolate: chocolate olive oil mousse
    249
    churros with chocolate 220–1

chorizo: baked eggs 69
  chickpea salad 84
  chorizo omelette 74
  chorizo pinwheels 207
  migas 205
  pasta with chorizo 177
  peasant's tortilla 70
  potatoes with chorizo 35
Christmas turkey 151–2
churros with chocolate 220–1
clafoutis: apricot clafoutis 231
clams: removing sand from 22
  beans with clams 190–1
  fish soup 22–3
  hake in green sauce 120
  paella 175–6
  sailor's clams 114
coca 188
cod: Basque cod 123
  Lent chickpeas 36
  peppers stuffed with cod 58
  salt cod omelette 68
courgettes: courgette fritters
    213
  courgette 'pasta' with prawns
    92
  courgette soup 30
  pasta bake 185
  pisto 194
cream cheese: ham and cheese roll
    212
croquetas 43–4
Cuban rice 180
cucumber: easy Mediterranean salad
    96
  gazpacho 29

D

damson jam 234

E

eggs 63
  apricot clafoutis 231
  baked 69
  chocolate olive oil mousse
    249
  chorizo omelette 74
  courgette fritters 213
  crispy fried egg 64
  Cuban rice 180
  empanada 53–4
  ensaladilla 48
  flan 253
  flavoured milk ice cream
    254
  French toast 219
  Iberian scrambled eggs 73
  leche frita 246
  mayonnaise 49
  nun's sighs 259
  orange and pomegranate pavlova
    238
  pancakes 218
  peasant's tortilla 70
  pisto 194
  safety of raw eggs 236
  salmon in *pepitoria* 127
  salpicón 128–9
  salt cod omelette 68
  snowy mountain 263
  stewed eggs 65
  strawberry mousse 234–5
  tomato and cheese loaf 217
  tortilla de patatas 66
  vinagreta 93
  yogurt mousse with cherries
    236
elephant ears 257
empanada 53–4
ensaladilla 48

F

feta cheese: chickpea salad 84
fideua with squid 179
fish 113
   Basque cod 123
   empanada 53–4
   ensaladilla 48
   fish soup 22–3
   fish stock 22
   fried hake 130
   hake in green sauce 120
   lemon sole 134
   Lent chickpeas 36
   mackerel pâté 140
   marmitako 117–18
   merluza a la gallega 139
   paella 175–6
   peasant's tortilla 70
   peppers stuffed with cod 58
   quick grilled fish 140–1
   roast fish 136
   salmon en croute 135
   salmon en papillote 124
   salmon in *pepitoria* 127
   salpicón 128–9
   salt cod omelette 68
   tuna salad 132
   tuna with tomato sauce 126
   see also seafood
flan 253
French toast 219
fritters: courgette fritters 213
fruit gums 199

G

gambas al ajillo 57
garden soup 26

garlic

garlic: chicken with garlic 146
   garlic prawns 57
   garlic soup 24–5
gazpacho 29
goat's cheese: winter salad 99
grapes: *migas* 205
green beans: beans with *ajoarriero* 80
green sauce 120
guacamole 208

H

hake: fried hake 130
   hake in green sauce 120
   merluza a la gallega 139
ham: baked eggs 69
   bolitas soup 32
   chard with ham 88
   croquetas 43–4
   ham and cheese roll 212
   Iberian scrambled eggs 73
   paella 175–6
   peasant's tortilla 70
   San Jacobos 163
   hojuelas 269
honey: aubergines with honey 87

I

Iberian scrambled eggs 73
ice cream 254

J

jam 233
   apple jam 225
   damson jam 234
   plum jam 233–4
jelly: fruit gums 199

L

lamb: roast lamb 155
    stewed lamb 156
leche frita 246
leeks: garden soup 26
    romesco sauce with roast leeks 83
lemon sole 134
lemonade 241
lemons: lemon curd muffins 264
    lemon posset 237
    lemonade 241
    quick grilled fish 140–1
    roast chicken 148
Lent chickpeas 36
lentejas 21
lentils: *lentejas* 21

M

macarrones con tomate 177
mackerel pâté 140
mayonnaise 49
egg-free mayonnaise 50
meatballs 186–7
Mediterranean salad 96
membrillo 229
meringues: orange and pomegranate
    pavlova 238
    snowy mountain 263
merluza a la gallega 139
merluza a la romana 130
merluza en salsa verde 120
migas 205
milk: egg-free mayonnaise 50
    flan 253
    flavoured milk ice cream 254
    leche frita 246
    milk buns 270
    rice pudding 255
    snowy mountain 263

mint: pineapple and mint salad
    242
monkfish: *salpicón* 128–9
mousse: chocolate olive oil mousse
    249
    strawberry mousse 234–5
    yogurt mousse with cherries 236
muffins: lemon curd muffins 264
mushrooms 100
mussels: paella 175–6
    tigres 46–7

N

nun's sighs 259

O

olive oil: chocolate olive oil mousse
    249
    olive oil cake 266
omelettes: chorizo omelette 74
    peasant's tortilla 70
    salt cod omelette 68
    tortilla de patatas 66
onions: coca 188
    garden soup 26
    pisto 194
    quick grilled fish 140–1
oranges: orange and pomegranate
    pavlova 238

P

paella 175–6
palmiers 257
pancakes 218
pancetta: *migas* 205
paprika: *merluza a la gallega* 139
    romesco sauce 83

parsley: hake in green sauce 120
partridges *estofadas* 150
pasta: *bolitas* soup 32
  easy pasta with bacon and peas
    182
  fideua with squid 179
  garden soup 26
  pasta bake 185
  pasta with chorizo 177
patatas a la importancia 103
pavlova: orange and pomegranate
    pavlova 238
peas: easy pasta with bacon and peas
    182
  peas with tomato sauce 104
peasant's tortilla 70
pepitoria: salmon in *pepitoria*
    127
peppers: Basque cod 123
  empanada 53–4
  ensaladilla 48
  Iberian scrambled eggs 73
  pasta bake 185
  peasant's tortilla 70
  peppers stuffed with cod 58
  pimientos de Padrón 55
  pisto 194
  roast peppers 91
  tuna salad 132
  vinagreta 93
picadillo 159
pig's cheeks in wine sauce 160–1
pimentón: *merluza a la gallega*
    139
  romesco sauce 83
pimientos de Padrón 55
pineapple and mint salad 242
pink lemonade 241
pinwheels: chorizo pinwheels 207
piquillo peppers: Basque cod 123

empanada 53–4
ensaladilla 48
Iberian scrambled eggs 73
peasant's tortilla 70
peppers stuffed with cod 58
tuna salad 132
pisto 194
pitta bread: easy Mediterranean salad 96
plum jam 233–4
pomegranate seeds: orange and
    pomegranate pavlova 238
poshed-up yogurt 250
pork: loin of pork 164
  picadillo 159
  pig's cheeks in wine sauce 160–1
  San Jacobos 163
  see also bacon; chorizo; ham; sausages
posset: lemon posset 237
potatoes: *ensaladilla* 48
  marmitako 117–18
  merluza a la gallega 139
  potatoes with chorizo 35
  quick grilled fish 140–1
  quick potatoes 101
  roast chicken 148
  roast fish 136
  self-important potatoes 103
  tortilla de patatas 66
prawns: courgette 'pasta' with
    prawns 92
  fish soup 22–3
  garlic prawns 57
  paella 175–6
  salpicón 128–9

Q

quesadillas 209
quince paste 229

R

rice: Cuban rice 180
    paella 175–6
    rice pudding 255
romesco sauce with roast leeks 83
Russian steaks 152–3

S

sailor's clams 114
salads: carrot salad 94
    chickpea salad 84
    easy Mediterranean salad 96
    ensaladilla 48
    tuna salad 132
    winter salad 99
salmon: salmon en croute 135
    salmon en papillote 124
    salmon in *pepitoria* 127
salmorejo 39
    aubergines with *salmorejo* 210
salpicón 128–9
salsa verde 120
salted cod: Lent chickpeas 36
    peppers stuffed with cod 58
    salt cod omelette 68
San Jacobos 163
sauces: *ajoarriero* 80
    apple sauce 224
    green sauce 120
    romesco sauce 83
    tomato sauce 78
    vinagreta 93
sausages: sausage bake 193
    see also chorizo
scones 258
scrambled eggs 73
seafood: beans with clams 190–1
    courgette 'pasta' with prawns 92
    fideua with squid 179

fish soup 22–3
fried squid 51
garlic prawns 57
hake in green sauce 120
paella 175–6
sailor's clams 114
salpicón 128–9
squid in its ink 119
tigres 46–7
tiny tortillas with shrimps 61
self-important potatoes 103
sherbet 198
shrimps: tiny tortillas with shrimps 61
snowy mountain 263
soup 19
    bolitas soup 32
    courgette soup 30
    fish soup 22–3
    garden soup 26
    garlic soup 24–5
    gazpacho 29
    Lent chickpeas 36
    lentejas 21
    potatoes with chorizo 35
salmorejo 39
spherifications 200
spinach: Lent chickpeas 36
squash *see* butternut squash
squid: fideua with squid 179
    fish soup 22–3
    fried 51
    paella 175–6
    squid in its ink 119
steak: grilled steak 160
    San Jacobos 163
strawberries: pink lemonade 241
    strawberry mousse 234–5
sweet potatoes: roast chicken 147
    Thai chickpeas 181

T

tapas 41
  croquetas 43–4
  egg-free mayonnaise 50
  empanada 53–4
  ensaladilla 48
  fried squid 51
  garlic prawns 57
  mayonnaise 49
  peppers stuffed with cod 58
  pimientos de Padrón 55
  ración 57
tigres 46–7
tiny tortillas with shrimps 61
Thai chickpeas 181
tomatoes: Basque cod 123
  coca 188
  Cuban rice 180
  easy Mediterranean salad 96
  gazpacho 29
  pasta bake 185
  pasta with chorizo 177
  peas with tomato sauce 104
  peppers stuffed with cod 58
  pisto 194
  quick grilled fish 140–1
  roast tomatoes 91
  romesco sauce 83
  salmorejo 39
  tomato and cheese loaf 217
  tomato sauce 78
tuna with tomato sauce 126
tortilla de patatas 66
tortillas (flatbreads): quesadillas
  209
tiny tortillas with shrimps 61
tortillas (omelettes): peasant's tortilla
    70
  tortilla de patatas 66
  tortillitas de camarones 61

tuna: empanada 53–4
  ensaladilla 48
  marmitako 117–18
  peasant's tortilla 70
  tuna salad 132
  tuna with tomato sauce 126
turkey: Christmas turkey 151–2

V

vinagreta 93
vodka: pineapple and mint salad 242

W

winter salad 99

Y

yogurt: poshed-up yogurt 250
  yogurt mousse with cherries 236
  yogurt spherifications 200

Epilogue

I have written this book to help me finance my involvement in a campaign for inspiring girls. But the reason I cook is three boys: my sons. And it is a slightly – just slightly – selfish reason.

You may feel you know me pretty well after reading the book. But what you probably do not yet know (or perhaps you have guessed) is how utterly protective I am of my kids. It really is not my fault, as it came with my genes: in the natural order of life there are mums… possessive mums… very possessive mums… extremely possessive mums… and then all the way at the very end there are Spanish mums! So much so that kids often live with us well into their thirties.

I know that at some point in life I will have to give my children the freedom to find their own paths, which is going to be – oh dear – so very tough. I am sure that, because I love them, I will – just like everybody else – get there.

But as they set up their own families and start sharing their lives with other women (or men) I hope they look back and say, as most sons in Spain do: 'Nobody cooks like my mother.'

Provided they think that, I am sure all will be well.

Acknowledgements

I owe my cooking to the wisdom, patience and generosity of all the amazing women in my family: my mother Mercedes; my aunts Mari Luz and Carmina; and my – sadly now dead – grandmothers María and Angela. My mother and aunts have helped me to fine-tune and double-test recipes and my aunt Loli has turned her house upside down looking for old photos. I am so very proud to be part of their family.

This book would not have been possible without the wonderful Nicky Ross, my totally trustworthy agent Annabel Merullo, the clever suggestions from Lucy Bannell, and the outstanding Hodder team, who have made it all so easy for me. In addition to being a fantastic publisher, Nicky gets the Most Courageous Editor Prize for daring to publish a cookery book written by no less than a lawyer.

A massive thanks to the fiercely loyal Begoña Lucena, my brain in the shadow, and to Tricia Carlin, without whom my life would simply collapse.

Thank you to my children – Antonio, Alberto and Miguel – for all the help with the cooking, the pictures, and for being my guinea pigs... but also for all their patience, as I was glued to my laptop writing this book during our family holiday in August 2015.

And finally the mother of all thanks to my husband Nick for his enthusiastic support, his good humour, his helpful suggestions (notwithstanding my frustrations with his censoring red pen) and his love. Travelling with you is a rollercoaster at times, but boy you know how to make life fun!

First published in Great Britain in 2016 by Hodder & Stoughton
An Hachette UK company

1

A CIP catalogue record for this title is available from the British Library

Hardback ISBN 978 1 473 63900 3
Ebook ISBN 978 1 473 63899 0

Editorial Director: Nicky Ross
Project Editor: Kate Miles
Editor: Lucy Bannell
Design & Art Direction: Nathan Burton
Photographer: Kris Kirkham
Photography Assistant: Hannah Hughes
Food Styling: Emily Jonzen
Food Styling Assistants: Poppy Mahon and Nicola Roberts
Props Styling: Lydia Brun
Props Styling Assistant: Lauren Miller
Shoot Producer: Ruth Ferrier
Proof reader: Annie Lee
Index: Caroline Wilding

Tiles provided by Bert & May, www.bertandmay.com

Printed and bound in Italy by Graphicom

Hodder & Stoughton policy is to use papers that are natural, renewable and recyclable products
and made from wood grown in sustainable forests. The logging and manufacturing processes are
expected to conform to the environmental regulations of the country of origin.

Hodder & Stoughton Ltd
Carmelite House
50 Victoria Embankment
London EC4Y 0DZ
www.hodder.co.uk